unsplintered

MIRA PRICE

To my brother, Arjun

CONTENTS

ACKNOWLEDGEMENTS

I would like to express my heartfelt appreciation to Mom, Dad and my brother, Rohan. Their unwavering love and support have been my constant source of strength.

I am ever indebted to my grandparents for their love, life lessons and blessings. I would also like to extend my thanks to my college professors, extended family and friends who have encouraged and supported me through the years.

Lastly, I join my palms in gratitude to Sai Baba. You are my master, guide, and protector. I am eternally thankful for your words that flow through my pen.

INSIDE THE LABYRINTH

OVIDII METAM. LIB. I.

OH MY DARLIN'

Oh my darlin',
Ain't got nothin',
While I have somethin'.

Time is flyin',
But I keep on tryin',
To stop her from cryin'.

Though I keep on lyin'
...to myself that she'll be okay.
But it's a mistake,
Cause she'll just run away,
Now I'll have to come in,
And save the day.

Oh my darlin',
Is workin',
To pay her bills,
And has stomachs to fill,
While she's already on the pill,
And not from her own will.

Oh my darlin',
Is savin',
All her earnin',
To make it for her children,
Who are forbidden,
To leave the den,

Cause they're just now bedridden.

Oh my darlin',
Is hurtin',
As she's beaten up till he's fed,
She turns blue and red,
While his opposers have fled,
And her children are coughin' up blood from the lead.

Oh my darlin',
Is steppin',
Into the poisonous chamber,
Where she becomes a flavour,
Where they've chained her,
And they bring another disrober that savours.

Oh my darlin',
Is sighin',
To see her little ones,
Her daughter and son,
Who are already dried up from that childlike fun,
And shall carry out tradition without bein' on the run.

Despite disease that's like havin' a life
…yet the livin' worth is none.

Oh my darlin',
Is smokin',
Like that's her only true right,
While she's too timid to just put up a fight,
She looks up into the sky of the night,
Hopin' and prayin' that she'll receive some light.

This is when she'll take her last breath,
That's gonna be like a megadeath.

Oh my darlin',
Will soon be dyin',
As her scars will not fade,
Even till they bury'er in shade.
Then all of this,
Will soon be displayed.

WHY DO ANGELS CRY?

My my, look at the sky, so beautiful and blue,
Clouds float in the sky, that's all they do.

Just imagine if you were an angel looking down from
    high,
You would feel the pain of the families of those who die.

The Innocent are taken by the seasons,
While they suffer as the rich justify their reasons.

Families admonish their children for defection,
While the young simply look for affection.

T.V. provides sensory images to feast,
While children die at the hands of the beast.

Who are those that don't care for the little one,
While they hold up their guns to the sun.

Foolish people with thoughts full of pride,
Yet innocence is now denied.

And now, all that is left is darkness and fears,
Mourning and sorrow fills the angel with tears.

So, let's make a stand and give into our rage,
Demanding the young have a voice on the stage.

DESERTIFICATION

Descendants of Great Thinkers of the past,
belittled to those with just blinkers as the Enlightened
    Ages diminished fast.

The Consecration of Capitalism,
With the onset of Digital Tourism.

The courtly Censorship,
The unruly One-Upmanship

...is what shrinks your souls to the size of a raisin.
Your tree of knowledge, too, dries up with resin.

You shrivel up into that sphere of safety,
While warping your own branches as rickety.

Your roots, short to even seep into soil,
So, you elongate those branches to embroil.

Your willows of wisdom,
Aren't even enough to perch one kingdom.

Even the sun shades its rays,
As all you factually desire are displays.

That is the plight of your own ignorance,
Towards those Palms of experience.
For you bury your bark in the dirt,
And head to the desert.

The oasis, your only refuge,
Unlike your delusions that drift as a deluge.

Now you wander the worthless seas of vanity,
And wonder how to survive this insanity.

As the Euphoric era of cyberspace,
A perilous place.

Vast like the sands of Arabia,
Becomes your next-door saviour.

The cacti have lost their spike and spine,
Osmosis opens pores but cannot prick a rigid opine.

The tumbleweed,
As withered as the witty seed.

The surrounding sensuous grass,
That you want to trespass.

Parched as you are,
You desire to travel wide and far.

So, in order to quench Curiosity,
You spread your wings with such velocity.

You arrive at the abyss of a voracious viper,
Which slithers to search for supper.

While, vultures, the vile creatures,
Wanting to prey on your fading features.

Yet still, with one eye to the sky, you hunt,
To sharpen your sword, you once called blunt.

You select and sort wielded weaponry,
As your wish is only to achieve blazonry.

The desert heat,
Enrages you to divide and defeat.

The infuriating information,
Turns into a toxic territorialization.

Colonies and imperial cities, established.
Profane pornographic phrases, published.

While the Web sags like the one of a spider,
As all abide by the inscriptions of the insider.

The treacherous tranquillizer, television,
Digs you a hole for hibernation.

For you slip into a reptilian slumber,
Which serenades your cerebrum as sombre.

The desert terrain,
Modified to be just as mundane.

For your innovation of the void,
Is the cause for your brain cells destroyed.

For even if you wanted to reach a new height,
(For that, Icarus despises your plight).

You chose to limit yourself in the lands of the limitless,
You are now viewed as visionless.

You shield yourself with a veil,
While you lie there, rotten and pale.

A dust storm approaches,
You cover your ears with cloches.

You lay there in the deserted sands of time,
With not even a footprint left behind.

The nightly chills cause an illusion,
To turn cold as ice and soon into oblivion.

The brilliant brains,
All abandoned and branded to be insane.

The philosophers of ole, the precious jewels,
Now look down upon us as fools.

FOOLISH ARISTOTLE

Aristotle, you defined tragedy as an:

"Imitation of an action that is serious, complete,
 and of a certain magnitude…
Through pity and fear effecting
the proper purgation of these emotions."

Tragedy is not a purgatory anymore, Aristotle.
It is not meant to invoke fear, a petty emotion.
It is meant to invoke excitement,
And arouse beasts out of their den.

The tragedies today,
Don't just have one climax, but several.
The fatal flaw is not simply because of falling into
 temptation,
But because of an arrogance seen in humanity.

The actions range from murder,
To planned assassinations.
From ordering one into suicide,
To mass genocide.

From slashing a slave,
To blowing up soldiers in a cave.
From crashing planes into buildings,
To children crushed under ceilings.

One after the other after the other,
This is what we encounter almost every day.
As these actions supposedly *immortalise* beings.
What happened to dying for glory as the true
    immortality now?

Like Homer's Achilles who no longer exists,
And perhaps, will never again see the light of day.
As the feature of his wrath,
Is the only relation to this world and the next.

Chaotic scenes that are depicted,
Time and time again in our tragedies, we call, 'news',
Are part of plots that link with reality.
Plots of peripeteia fall from fortune into misfortune
    every minute.

Anagnorisis, the awareness seen in the media,
Of learned characters who only contemplate,
With an extra touch of 'Aparneomaisis',
A state of stasis, due to the depths of denial.

As fires of opposing beliefs engulf the city,
The protagonists in the plot prefer to sit and watch the
    city burn.
Rome has not been the only town up in flames,
As all are tempted to take up arms in fits of anger.

Characters who strongly hold onto their opinions,
Before even opening the Gates of Outlook.
These same characters mimic each other,
Like Plato rightly said, this imitation is twice removed
    from reality.

And as Albert Bandura observed the imitation,
Characters pick up on illogical conspiracies,
For these fools have no mind of their own.
Blatant statements based on *observations* incite all to
    imitate others.

They pick up their sword, their gun, their bombs and
    knives,
And this is coupled with strategic crimes,
To disembark protesters and dismember artsy visionaries.
Atrocities continuously occur to cover the white flag
    with crimson.

The real tragedy, when the observed is repeated in action,
Like a vicious cycle till all are accustomed to death.
Rendering us as heartless and mindless,
As the savage beasts that lurk around at every bent corner.

Do you see their repentance and regret?
As seen in Achilles,
Who wept wildly in remorse,
For sending his companion to the battlefield…

Only to know the angels of Destined Death
Were sending Patroclus out on his last fight?
No. Today, it is all about that shining armour,
Those tanks that harbour and the medallions of valour.

And as the tragic war begins,
To fight the outsider of an enemy,
The covert battlefield within,
Is what truly shatters one's walls down.

As for the diction, Aristotle, note this headline-
"Young girl and old woman,
Raped and drowned to death in a bathtub,
By enemy forces."

The froth bubbles in this bloody bath,
As the commander induces an overflow.
Indulgence in lust turns the blood acidic,
For they both drown in this bloody acid.

The irony of defining the inexplicable!
Such literary devices are used in today's tragedies.

Language, surely a useful mode of communication.
Enunciation made loud and clear but silenced by a
    victim's screams.

A temporary relief, melody in mournful tones of
    melancholy.
The families of victims, crying.
There is neither a major chord that vibrates nor one that
    is sung.
For those terrified but sacrificial souls remain unsung.

The spectacle of it all is what is enjoyed the most,
Tragic moments like these, beneficial to businesses.
Profits driven by imparting commercials inciting panic,
To further the interests of individual governments.

In this, you were right, Oh Aristotle!
Panic is what consumers and characters are both based
    on,
As they purge themselves onto screens,
And fear the worst, afraid of association and affectation.

Catharsis selfishly gratifies all characters,
Where each character believes,
That they are the protagonist of their own story,
And that they have full control over their lives.

Today's tragedies, therefore,
Structured almost like yours, oh Aristotle.
Differentiated by the intensity of deadly disasters,
That are a result of our current affairs.

Aristotle,
The tragedy that you suggested was twice removed from
    today's reality,
And this imitative instinct is indeed the harsh actuality.
The only hope one holds on to, is a reversal in fate,
Which with the correct lenses, can help turn back all
    into an illusion.

ARE YOU TRULY HUMAN?

You say you are members of the human race,
And you have the audacity to call yourself human?

When these disfigured men touch my trunk,
As if they seek pleasure,
They seek pleasure by touching a woman's breast,
Now these dirty hands touch my chest!

The very roots that held me strong,
Didn't keep me grounded for too long,
The very earth that had forever been under my feet,
Slips away as if they are lured by torture and deceit.

My limbs that you touch leave marks,
Marks that cannot be washed away,
Just like that little girl being afraid of the dark,
For the fear that unwanted hands will touch her for play.

I expect the fresh water gives me purity,
Yet I feel like the nebulous inside is mired.
Even my breath cannot be of surety,
As you choke me and I have no place to hide.

The air was my only friend,
As I greeted her by swaying out of joy.
Now I cry out for help,
While she says she is just playing coy.

Marvellous fruits and flowers bloom,
Like the children of the dawn.
For now, they resemble the womb,
Which beguiles you like the moon.

The moon which you inject into your body,
Is the poison that brings out elicitation,
And this ecstasy of yours leads to my tragedy.
Though you educate your people to illiteracy

…as the conspiracy unfolds in this allegory.

I am shredded down into bits and pieces,
Or forced to drown in your faeces.
I am burnt alive like a widowed wife.
While I wish you had stabbed me with a knife.

My remembrance of this – omnified.

And even my remains won't be spared,
The incineration of my corpse will be denied any sort of
    respect defiled,
As you fight for the rest of my kin,
Which is left unconquered to sin.

The circle of life, which was meant to connect,
All species in their diversity,
Now a hexagonal curve showing all forms of disrespect,
Where the equality shared is all gone.

Where there is no time to introspect.
While you yourselves believe to be the human space,
And you believe you are no longer primitive,
You choose to call yourselves civilized.

Are you really human?
Or do you just value your place?

TRUE DEFORMITY

Once upon a time,
My body was
A fortification of fortitude,
Against infertility of all kinds.

My curves, my nerves,
My birthmarks, my stretch marks,
My moles, my holes,
My organs, my scars,

Were all islands,
Clustered together,
To form the mainland, the heart,
Interlinked with the masterful mastermind.

The roots, our veins,
As complex as the nexus of a tree,
The structure, our spinal cord,
Just like the base of a tree trunk.

The topography, the most rustic,
In a humble environment,

Which caressed me as a new babe,
With the love as pure as of a mother.

For the womb usually becomes a home,
Surrounded by bodily fluids,
Which naturally nurtures the process,
That further illustrates the Intended Design.

It is later that frailty transforms the pupa,
Into a more mature sturdy self,
To withstand the flimsiness of time.
My life becomes just a game to you.

The axe you carry in your hands,
Cuts my beautiful growing tree,
Into a stump, stunting my growth,
Till the end of my time.

You chop my body based on proportion,
Like a butcher to the limb of a lamb.
You place my body on your examination table,
And add lights to blind me into disorientation.

My head, my hands,
My calves, my feet,
My breasts, my thighs,
My eyes, my arms,

All critiqued by your kind,
In the examination of life.
All ridiculed by your kind,
Like the ridiculous acts of a circus animal.

That shrink my soul to follow the path of sin,
That led me to you, the Devil's doorstep,
To picture my perfection in your eyes,
Pleasure takes over pain.

Plath stated it right.

I do become your *"Magnum Opus"*,
As you become my conductor,
While I writhe in pain and fight in vain,
Just like the beast on display.

"I turn and I burn,"
And once you're through with me,
I become the plastic,
That you so moulded into a straw.

My face, disfigured,
My curve, straightened,
My complexion, whitened,
My mind, disheartened.

The volcanoes erupt within.
Fissures fill the oceanic floor.

Cracks and crevices isolate islands.
Deforestation depletes my very own soil.

Meanwhile, I hand you a large sum,
Emptying my pockets,
As your generous reward,
To my physical deformation.

For shattering my idealistic dreams.
For breaking up my bodily remains.
For depleting the very water from my ground.
For polluting my very own plains.

I land up in a landfill, full of toxins,
Like the non-biodegradable straw,
That either collects on the surface,
Or floats in the seas below it.

As my body cripples from within,
I find myself suffocating the other,
As my mind drowns in deadly poisons,
While I float in tragic piles of trash.

Whilst I breathe, whilst I eat,
I become used to being examined,
Under that blinding limelight every day,
Like the circus creature in a cage.

How dare you call my land infertile?
How dare you change nature's course manually?
How dare you design it all artificially?
How dare you torment all to commit such an atrocity?

For your axe,
Single-handedly destroyed humanity,
You, with the eye of an Opportunist,
Bred *"Beauty"*, out of deformity.

DEATH IN AGONY

For us, a burning sorrow,
For Death, a sulking shadow.

Death, too, yearns for the past tense,
But is bound to wind heartbeats up like clockwork, at
    its own expense.

Wrinkled, sagging corpses left all alone.
Wreathed skulls, interwoven with woe.

Breaths, barren, with dry coughs of blood.
Tumours, tubers, a warzone with tar-like mud.

Broken bones and bloody bodies rust,
Dragged at dusk across the dust.

Parasites praise the ruin,
With sweet swallows, hollowing out a human.

The honeycombs of our tomb,
Glorious, yet holes fill the womb,

Till fires are fed to consume the spine,
As organs turn oblivious to time.

Oh poor, ill-disposed Death,

You ought to be considered considerate and bittersweet,
As you reveal one's departing retreat.

White, as pure as your summoning stairway,
Unlike the doctored doors of doomsday.

It is you who saves each one with dignity,
As you lay to rest the dead and diseased in a place of
        sanctity.

You quietly lull to sleep, or prick like a thorn, but never
        a needle that prolongs the pain,
For it was your duty to protect all from treatments of
        the inhumane.

Your death-approaching awareness,
Jolts one to awaken from the nights of unconsciousness.

Writings honour your worth and abode,
Elegies write themselves as a Deathly Ode.

But oh! The horror! The horror! Oh, the horror!

The sheer significance of your being,
Is quite unlike versions we have seen.

Dearest Death,

It is your heart that aches and stains,
While a drowsy numbness pains.

It is rather your warm welcomes which we hear,
That soothe your dull cold ear.

It is rather you who can scarcely cry
"Weep! Weep! Weep! Weep!"

For your duty stops,
when you serenade yourself to sleep, to sleep, to sleep, to
     sleep.

It is you who kindly cannot stop any longer,
When your heart grows for one soul fonder.

For the world anticipates your removal,
Retributive Justice shall never seek your approval.

Your watchful eye, your angelic wings that fly,
Are not enough to save an innocent soul from the Lie.

As we prick the soul to be sold,
These are curtains of life you are forced to fold.

Oh! The tragedy that hath befallen,
As all your rights hath been stolen!

The sincere dedication to your duty,
In the hands of humans who demand deputy.

I shall mourn for you, Death.

For it is the pompous policies of our kind,
Merely to vindicate the scientific find.

We hoard the organ to hunt for the wound,
While the cause is merely assumed.

Merciless be our methods of murder,
Till one obtains The Order.

You hover, fostering fumes and flames,
But the pyre is lit only after we finish the game.

The grave is in grave despair,
For we sentence thousands to death in pairs.

Death, your figure is fading,
Your light is shading.

Death, where did you dissipate?
Are you all but a dream that syncopates?

For it is rather we who have heard or read,
Beautiful tales imagined but never implicated for the
    dead.

It is rather our senses which have been dead a thousand
    years,
As we woefully write this for our future seers.

It is rather we who turn to those liars, the candles, and
    the moon,
Instead of swallowing the truth, a lagoon.

Dark Mother and Lord, who is always gliding near with
    soft feet,
Why must you choose to fade in this floating ocean of
    obsolete.

Death, you victorious spirit and guide,
May God be with you, on the other side!

References used:
1. An Ode to A Nightingale by John Keats
2. Endymion by John Keats
3. An Elegy Written in the Country Churchyard by Thomas Gray
4. The Chimney Sweeper by William Blake
5. Because I Could Not Stop for Death by Emily Dickinson
6. To a Poet a Thousand Years Hence by James Elroy Flecker
7. Mirror by Sylvia Plath
8. Death Carol by Walt Whitman

THE FALL OF MAN

Encouraging perspectives,
to be deceptive.

Reinstating phonies,
to the positions of appraisal.

Deploying detectives,
to cover up the works of the Worldly order.

Electing politicians whose motto is solely the pursuit of
    power,
And not happiness.

Uprising, not the voices that hollow themselves into
    oblivion,
But the farcical qualities of questioning.

Presenting a villainous character as charismatic,
While their reflexes are aristocratically autocratic.

Treating treachery as if the very fur and skin of this
	faded figure is to be revered,
Is nothing but a pity on humanity!

Shame on you! Shame on all of us!
We have put ourselves into this misery,

Where the world is quasi-judicial,
And superficial.

Where the world is biased,
But supposedly pious.

Where the world is penanced,
But also silenced.

And repressed,
And depressed.

Where the world is dehumanized,
And catastrophized.

To behave in ways of the discriminatory,
And predatory.

And fanatic,
But not diplomatic.

And authoritative,
To conserve the conservative.

And radicalist,
And fundamentalist.

Till all are guiltless,
And hopeless

...Is a result of this humanity.

Terrible are the times we live in, where hope only comes
        from an external element,
And not one which has internal resonance.

The fear that God will not show mercy on our poor souls

...are what subject humans to victimhood,
But also leads all to preach Prophethood.

The terror that struck the perishing public,

Is it really necessary?
Or is it, by all means, a way to make a mark on one's
        own territory?

The haunting horrors of the past are horrors of hysteria,
And of mad imperia.

How then, do we rid ourselves of such a past,
If all we think of till now is when will we breathe our
    very last?

We pitiful creatures-

Have devastated,
Have depleted,

Have shambled,
Have scrambled,

Have been defeated and fleeted,
Have interrogated rather than contemplated,

Have recited that ignited,
Have inflicted and indicted,

Have tightened and quietened,
All that this preservative planet has to offer.

At one point in time,
You called yourselves to be at the Centre of the Universe.

Now that you realize that those were the notes of
    Narcissus,
The self-identity that you clung onto so dearly has
    dispersed.

Philosophical thought is the only discourse,
Which appreciates the truth.

Socratic, then Platonic,
Machiavellian and Hobbesian,

Nihilism, Freudian and Bandurian,
All of them have proof,

That humanity is doomed,
For eternity.

And there is no other entity,
Unless we clear that sacred path of sanctity,

That exists between God and Man,
Else we'll all forever be damned.

Women are the seductress, like Eve,
Because they conceive,

A son, a daughter to please,
And because they believe...in humanity.

Female foeticide, a serious thing,
For it is the blood that rubs against their ring.

Yet still, they bring into this world,
A precious pearl, that rotted till death and is later forgotten.

You think God would humbly take back their gift given
    to you?
Why must you humans be hypocrites while listening to
    hymns on the bayou?

Making a demon out of God won't help,
Yet, making a God out of a demon won't help either.

Scriptures are the one true source of sin,
Acting God is the needle and the pin.

Taking a godman's words in literal meaning,
To separate lovers apart from christening.

Or to oppress officials in office,
So as to beatify the polis.

All of this-

To defy,
To petrify,

To terrorize,
To immortalize,

To force,
To endorse,

To speculate,
To flagellate.

Must the need arise,
Before the sunrise,

A cacophony, a procession,
That turns obsessions into confessions?

Must a staunch believer and "receiver" have the need to
    antagonize,
And galvanize?

As the Gods in heaven shall value their *honourable duty*?
Isn't this a duty more to do with one over another man's
    deputy?

What sort of urge or desire,
Must you have to selectively send thousands of bodies to
    that funeral pyre?

Be it of woman, or child or woman with child,
Or of innocent souls whose damnation is filed?

Are you demons in human form?
Or humans in demon form?

So must you not use these words to possess the
    "Almighty's soul",
For your kind would be to the Devil himself sold.

Must a fire conflagrate the corners of a home,
So that God can protect your own?

God need not be summoned like a slave,
After all, it is the choice of God to pardon or not to
    pardon even the souls of the depraved.

You revere a soul as bold as God.

On one hand, humans achieve godlike superiority,
On the other, you make God's supreme soul itself an
    inferiority.

Wicked and cunning are your thoughts, must I say,
And then, you complain, there is no one to save the day?

This is nothing but a pity on humanity.

The greatest sin and the fall of man,
Therefore, to make God… a human.

ON NATURE

GRIEF

As I walk home one night,
This eerie sound caught my attention,
That was let out by the turning on of a light,
Here, I feel a cold sensation.

I creep towards the shadows,
For I then hear shrill and loud screams.
I see nothing but dark meadows,
As if I was a part of some terrifying dream.

As a torch was lit, to my horrific shock,
Of seeing traces of blood that had been slain,
All across the rock.
My heart was dreading with pain.

At the sight of a mangled body that lay near my feet,
It took some time for me to recognize,
Till I reached out for a seat.
Oh! Look at Nature's tragic demise!

I lay near her, traumatized, shivering, trembling,
With a sense of guilt.

Emitting sounds of groaning and grumbling,
All that was left was the silt.

For all the pleasant flowers that had to bloom,
For all the innocent animals that she had to rear,
For all the delicious fruits that had to ripen soon,
For all the fruitful trees she considered so dear.

For all the precious waters came as one,
For all that she had yet to offer,
This was all that had been done,
While we were filling up our coffers.

She began to rumble with the thunder, shake with the
    tremor,
Roar with the wind, shriek with the water quite often,
Until she was murdered like some began to endeavour,
Now, she lay in her coffin.

SLEEP SOUNDLY MY CHILD

Sleep soundly, my child!

For the world will eventually fall to darkness,
Just like the darkness that envelopes even the evil eye.

Sleep soundly, my child!

For the world sleeps while you are on guard.
Your prayers to protect all are heard.

Sleep soundly, my child!

For the world will pay for their sins.
They will soon be orphaned just as you were.

The world has surely caught its prey.
Their trap, like a spiralling web.

Little do they know,
They are part of a larger nexus.

Sleep soundly, my child!

For your metamorphosis was skipped,
Like a fast-forward button played on your life.

Your innocence snatched away from you,
Like a woman stripped of clothes, ashamed.

Your presence, which is in absence,
From all those who truly cared for you.

Sleep soundly, my child!

For your rest is well deserved,
I shall not pester you by making you relive your past.

The reassurance from my side should help,
So, rest your weary head and lay faith in me.

For I only ought to put my point across,
To those delirious actors and silent readers.

Now I shall get up and say to the rest,

The tragedies of living with an adulterous adult,
And the sacrifices made to pubescence.

Exposures of paedophilia and their pleasures,
The constant enticements without censures.

Have you ever thought of the daily traumas?
Have you ever pondered for even a minute on these evils?

To the rest,

If not the guardians, then who are you?
If not the caretakers, then what are you?

Why do you choose to lust over little ones?
Why do you choose to feed your own greed and not
    their hungry feeble mouths?

They are just my harmless children,
What did they do to deserve this torture?

To the rest,

You are all as hollow if you just sit back,
And press play on the horror movie ahead.

The silenced screams are not enough,
To keep you at the edge of your seat.

The pitchforks ready to behead a newborn,
While you chew and crunch on treats.

To the rest,

The mysterious disappearances thrill you.
The bloodied floors surprise you.

How can you be human?

Are you the ghoul we are meant to fear?
Can you see ignorance on your doorstep now?

Or are your window curtains still drawn,
To hide your place in reality?

Mark my words!

One day, the sunlight will burn you,
Till you see that ray of truth.

One day, the fires that you so like to gorge on,
Will melt your flesh and bone.

One day, the blood-red sky will make you cry,
Till the blood blinds you bare.

One day, the dawns of destiny,
Will mean your dusk as you turn to dust.

So, sleep soundly my child!
Trust in me as you lay in my arms.

Rest easy, oh dear one!
For the rest will be sent to their own doom.

YOU SHALL RISE AGAIN

You shall rise again,
At the darkest hour,
In the heightened dusk,
Looking at the devilish moon,
Where you transform.

You shall rise again,
At the sight of mangled corpses,
With dreadful groans,
Amidst the frightening fog,
Where all that surrounds you turns into dust.

You shall rise again,
To slay all that approaches you.
To put all to rest.
To endanger those treasured lives.
Where you find one to counter.

The one who emits a whitish light.
The one who preaches about the path of harmony,
The one who spreads the warm rays of the sun.
The one who understands all.
The one who fades these dark shadows away.

You shall rise again,

Where this fellow being rises to become a God.
As he heals your wounds,
And he fills your inner core with love,
As he saves all from you,
And he removes the evil eye.

But you shall rise again,

For you will always find ways to re-enter this realm.
For you will always create sins or troubles.
For you will always bring fear along with you.
Though many rebels will go against you,
And you will be defeated by a new one each time,

You will forever be remembered as the "Demon".
But oh, you shall rise again.

As mortals mightn't understand,
For you are also a part of the balance.
You are a necessity in making the one.
You are a form that saves the world.
For you also give reasons to living ones as to why you
    must be extinguished.

So, you shall rise again!

PROPHECY

We are the Daughters of the Dead,

Here to convey a message,
That your lives are at risk.
You'll feel your perception in vain.
You'll run to Deception in pain.

Resolution and Respite will only be hoisted,
When the destitute tear down that flag.
Until then, your hypocrisy,
Will continue to enrage.

We are The Daughters of the Dead,

You must survive-
The overcast,
The storm,
And the flood.

Your powerless fiends fight,
Your powerful friends light the fire.

As forgery becomes the fuel,
Drudgery falls into hands of the peasantry.

We are The Daughters of The Dead,

As Disease wracks brains,
While some wielded as sceptics,
Governments disorient personas,
As forces tighten restrictions.

Departure of lives lead to bribes,
Prostitutes protect those,
Who mind and mint their own money.
Pride believes in himself as a martyr.

We are the Daughters of The Dead,
And are here to warn you.

Nature is too good for you all,
You have destroyed every face of it,
Every place of it,
With your wicked smile.

We prophesize a world,
That all humans will soon dread.
So, make it easier for yourselves,
By turning luck against time.

We, the Daughters of The Dead,
Believe these fallen souls,
Rise to serve a new Queen.

The new Queen shall arise-

From the depths of the Oceans of Orion,
From the shadows of the sun,
From the refractions of the rain,
From fissures that create the canyons' cave.

She will be the Daughter of Death,
And the Mother of Men.
Born from neither Venus nor Mars,
But Earth.
Only she shall be our New Queen.

This new Queen shall descend,
From the hellish heavens.
Bathed in Brutes' blood,
Who hath boast of his betrayal.

Wearing drapes of death around her neck,
Pierced with twigs of their funeral pyre.
Accessorized with wrist wreaths of woe,
Cloaked with skulls and spleens.

A new Queen shall preside-

To deploy destructive forces,
And employ heartless ones by her side.
To mortify merciless murderers,
Who are the self-proclaimed altruists.

The barbaric beasts,
Will be hunted down.
The protective priests,
Must renounce all relations with The Renowned.

Restorative Justice,
Is her response.
To those who punish her for wearing the crown,
Such will be the mighty forces of our Queen.

To protect the ones,
Who walk The Deserts of despair.
And the paths taken by predators,
To guide them to salvation.

She shall decide,
The course of time.
Either an apocalyptic annihilation,
Or miraculous mirth.

For this Queen shall not require a King.

The game of chess, chance, and destiny,
Well played by the Head of Horoscopes,

Shall lie with the Leviathan,
Our Queen.

The unstable Universe,
Wields the Wands of Worth,
And Books of Bones,
And Spells of Silence.

A new Queen, therefore, shall arise-

To stabilize like a Sensei,
With the cumulative energies of the cosmos,
The sins of nature,
Shall also return to the hounds of hell.

We are The Daughters of The Dead,
And we prophesize a New Queen.

THE PURE ELEMENTS

The sea waves can be as mighty as a sword,
Yet as tranquil as a life-giving Lord.

The sea waves are a symbol of fighters,
Yet also signify dreamers.
The sea waves watch us fall,
Yet still also gives us time to crawl.

Its' water an eternal element,
That gives nutritional supplements,
To each and every biotic resource,
While it travels along its course.

It does not pay heed to those who plead for mercy,
As it brings out destruction that all must see,
Though it supports ones who truly desire to lay inside
    its womb,
Who sees the hazy light rays and the dark tomb.

For they are sent down,
As they will never drown,

And they all also combine to form nature's crown,
Yet these creatures will suffer due to some who
    continuously frown.

The pure element of Water,
Can be a saver as well as a slaughterer,
So one must give back water its' honour,
For it has more than just valour.

The ball of fire that is called "The Sun",
Is a source of not only light but heat like other than none.
The sun rays reflect as per the laws of science,
And the universal law – is to lead without defiance.

But the fury that the fiery hell can unleash,
With fumes that sometimes never cease.
The pleasure that one receives from this warmth,
Can also put an end to a new dawn.

Flames lit with vibrant shades of red,
That many seem to dread,
As it captures one's sight from far distances.
It donates its blood for a cold-blooded one's sustenance.

Yet it burns all down into ashes,
And leaves wounded marks of the violent slashes.
It believes in the virtue of giving justice in the form of
    acts of outrage,
But can also be as wise as a sage.

Messing with the trail of the fire element,
May just mean a curse from the underground to become
    resonant,
And spew balls ignited at extreme high temperatures.
For many, it will cost their huge expenditures.

Bodies that have been melted away,
Will soon become an evil source of display.

However, a charmer such as that of the "Maple Tree",
Whose roots are held tight, yet still can be free,

To be attractive to a huge degree,
While one admires its beauty even when on a spree.

A spiritual folk,
Is that one called "The Oak",
Who is mature way beyond its years whenever it spoke,
And is the hub for wisdom that will croak.

The lair of the green land where no soul is tethered,
Where all are the friends of ether,
Love intensifies by the gifts offered by its assistance,
If one understands the true meaning of its existence.

It is one who wishes to bring equality among all energies,
Who wants all to emerge as synergies,
But also writes genealogies,
For all, as life's treasured philosophies.

The soil is just the beginning,
To all beautiful forms of designing,
And doesn't leave not one confining,
For all the seeds end up christening.

It remains dependent on the rest of the fundamental core,
That support its life such as the transparent elixir or
Air and water for nurturing and feeding it more,
And the sun, for keeping it warm.

But when it roars and rumbles,
It provides impetus to terrifying troubles,
That leave every living being in shock,
As they can shatter into tiny rubble, even a rock.

Treat oh must one treat a figure that is shady,
As a generous lady,
All is blessed with an antibody,
And one shall prepare a rhapsody.

The last and final source of godliness,
Is that of Air without which would turn one breathless.

The lively and energetic flair,
Is that of Air,
Who was a breeding ground,
Who seems to be in despair.

One transpires the fragrant odour,
And one feels a breeze that is colder,
With such delicacy and intricacy,
It handles all with accuracy.

It searches for a leaf in its presence not swayed,
But without it, all seem to be as still as when displayed.
The gushing and swirling wind,
Breaks every little piece that one can find.

Where it shrieks and howls when it is hungry for revenge,
Till it is left unchallenged.
Before it used to harmonise a melodious song,
Now it is forced to bring dust and dirt along.

It can become one's worst enemy,
Yet will still be an alchemy,
By mending a depressive dichotomy,
That ought to be considered blasphemy.

Its' pristine glory is its ability to render moral service,
In the form of setting up a hospice,
Where it carries one's dying breath till they reach its
    absence,
And where all bodily remains are blown away into
    transience.

The main spirits without which life could not sustain,
Oh, I beg all not to leave these heavenly forms in disdain.

For these are all parts of clarity and purity,
That cleanse surroundings with their divinity,
Acknowledge them in places of serenity,
And respect them with humility.

Oh, Dearest mother and father,
Spare your children from the future disaster.
I have enlightened them rather,
Let them decipher how to work till they become their
     own masters.

ROCK BOTTOM

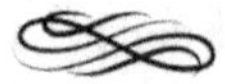

You hide yourself,
From this world,
Like a caterpillar in a cocoon,
Yet pretend to seek help,
From another,
Like taking shelter on a pleasant noon.

You think that all is written in death and decay,
All that pleases you turns into dismay.
You weep for hours on end,
Like living in a complete tragedy,
You can't seem to shape a bend
…Anymore as your spirit is broken but your heart
    desires a remedy.

You think that the world is crashing and crumbling down,
Like you are going to drown,
In the deepest of waters,
Till you turn cold and numb,
Just like that of a slaughterer,
As you think you have had to succumb

…Succumb to your inner devil,
That calls out for dread,
Though you choose to remain civil,
To the one who leaves you misled.
This is where you think you've hit rock bottom,
You find the solution to none

…To none of the complex conundrums of life.
You lay on your bed, helplessly pondering over what
    could have been,
You feel emotions as intense as the heat from the sun,
This is where you think you have hit rock bottom,
When suddenly, you realize there must be another,
Who suffers terribly with all sorts of the symptom

…but are forced to drain it out due to the brain drain
…or because they fear they will be labelled *insane*.
The scorching heat,
May leave a little scar on your body,
But will take away the other's feet,
They walk with skin peeling as they must live in jeopardy.

The wrestling mania,
Over something to eat,
Is nothing like how you get the scrumptious treat,
Though you might have insomnia,
They pick up the dirt till one has been beat,
Then snatch from each other, like suffering from
    kleptomania.

The deadly disasters,
May have destroyed you,
The bothersome disorders,
May have wrecked you,
Though you would be called an imposter,
If you saw what they had gone through.

These are indeed the ones who hit the rock bottom.
So must you not complain,
Of the mountains, you make out of a molehill,
Or the fires that you entice yourself to fall into.
For you are the one with all the gain,
And not the one with all the pain.

I AM DONE

Listen up!
Cause I'm not going to repeat myself!

I'm done!
I'm done with constantly being tugged in different
    directions,
Like a twisted rope that bends
…till I tear apart and all that is left are strewn threads.

I'm done with being critiqued by those who choose to
    miscomprehend
…my Art, all for the 'feeling' of being the intellectual folk.
Like the Picasso who no one could ever understand,
For his kind are very special yet despised with every
    stroke.

I'm done with humans overriding someone's right to
    breathe,
That is against my moral positions,
Like the police officer who had to decide,
Whether to let him breathe or push his knee into his
    neck till he dies.

I'm done with enacting a farce falling into traps,
To capture the sentimental spectacle,
Like a toddler crying for attention from a multitasking
    mother,
Which is all for the lens of camera.

Or a convict who convinces the court of his innocence,
While still being a threat to everyone's existence,
All under the cloak of a lodger,
Who caresses the silk, to further his pestilence.

I'm done dealing with malicious personalities,
Who manipulate my potential simply by stroking
    conscience,
As if sympathy is part of the process of hypnosis,
Synonymizing scars with wounds of self-fulfilling
    prophecies.

I'm done with hiding from my own being,
Like throwing a synthetic blanket to a flame,
Hoping to extinguish the truth that lies within my soul,
Underneath all those engulfed layers, I feel a wreck, as if
    I'm the one to blame.

I'm done seeing demons dressed up as saints,
With denial as a mechanism of self-defence,
Like mud piled up upon more mud,
To conceal the truth, a sinkhole.

I'm done with role models having to hide their insecurities,
Like keeping their guards intact.
For fear that the world will despise them at their worst,
So, they must keep up with their pact.

I'm done with the ungrateful affluent,
Who take pride in diagnosing themselves with disease,
Feeding the business by becoming the hypochondriac
      they weren't destined to be.
Meanwhile, howls of help by the destitute don't make
      the front page.

I'm done with society's hegemony over who experiences
      pain,
As if suppressing emotion wasn't enough,
By dousing it down with drink and pill,
For society alone is desolate and numb.

I'm done equating depression with sadness,
Out of respite for not fitting into what society labels 'the
      norm',
Or out of finding newer identification through labels,
All because I fail to simply see my existence outside of
      them.

I'm done with playing the victim when I know I ain't one!
I need to rise from the shadows I threw myself in,
And begin by looking at the little things in life,
To see that whatever I am, whoever I am, is more than
      enough!

I'm done being the Nihilist in my own life,
When I can be the Optimist!
Good deeds are with the intent of being selfish.
But who cares?

As long as it heals hopeless souls and revives humanity,
To remind us of our branches as much as our roots,
Then who am I to resist change?
Why must I despise the art of living?

I'm done…with playing dead!

WHERE THE TRUTH LIES

SEARCH FOR THE TRUTH

I search for a sign,
A vision,
A memory of mine,
A voice of precision.

Where is the truth hiding?

Why am I denied my rights?
Yet still left with no answers of it subsiding,
While it continues the bloody fights?
When will the truth come out?

I must search for the truth.

I search the skies,
The shadows,
The past times where all dies,
The battles.

Where is the truth hiding?
Why mustn't I join the pieces of an unsolved mystery,

That you assume I use rules of *"yours"* for abiding?
Why shouldn't I know it is an act of wicked sorcery?

I search the depth below,
The fallen yet mysterious underworld,
The monstrous rivers yet to flow,
The troublesome chiefs that have been so far unfurled.

Yet no answer from any fact has been derived,
And possibly, there will never be one.
As I suppose this all has been undermined,
For what clearly has been done.

To breed the criminals under your feet,
And then cry out for help when they turn against all,
When you allow them to take your seat,
As one of a minister that cannot fall.

Where is the truth hiding?
But if I must search for the truth,
I dare to ask-
Why has the truth been hiding?

TRUTH, WHERE DO YOU PREVAIL?

Where is mine eye,
that converses with the *"I"*?
Where is time and why does he prefer to pry?
Shall it not be the precedence over the Lie?

Where is the one who accompanies the noble dictum of
    valour?
Why must you mirror the Lady of Justice, but with a
    frail pallor?
For all yearn to possess her sense of vigour,
Though you choose to let it devour.

Where pose you, Truth, this fancy figure of art?
Whose magnificent design is held by a rampart,
Yet this lady is blind even from the heart,
Who speaks, yet in a tone that cannot separate the two
    ladies apart.

Where possibly must Truth prevail,
On the books of account, law, and tale?
Or on the holy priests and their trail,
Where do we see her presence fail?

Truth, a possibility,
Yet higher her liability.
Prospects of proposal dishevel her stability,
As she responds to those who doubt her ability.

Her ability to tear down to bits till every bit of shackle
    burns,
To enunciate all that one earns,
All happen with Truth's allegiance to the consciousness-
    filled urns,
The wisdom as a prop, where memory switches its side
    to spurn.

Truth, a worthy suit of honour,
She shall become the dignified owner,
Though she also lures the loner,
To indulge in *"blasphemous"* behaviours of humour.

Succumb a lively soul,
To the gates of Truth of ole,
And they shall lie in the guilty arms that cajole,
Truth, we know you have concealed the scroll.

Justice prevails,
Yet Truth derails,
They say – *"Justice has been served"*,
Why then, can there not ever be a Truth served?

For Truth, we all aspire to acquaint ourselves with you,
Our mind and heart are a tussle to listen to,
We, on our quest for self-knowledge, is true,
So where does Universal Truth lie, for us to pursue?

IS THE TITLE REALLY NECESSARY?

Is a title really necessary?

When you already know that this poem will be all about
    the dark times,
And random rhymes.

About fading memories,
Or the worlds of contemporaries.

About tragic moments,
Or heartbreaking components.

About social stigmas,
Or platonic enigmas.

About placid crimes,
Or violent mimes.

About historical drama,
Or about the perfect panorama.

About the ideal living fantasy,
Or about the realistic apostasy.

Is the title really necessary?

When scenic visions occur,
On a simple parchment of paper.

As your mind travels the distance,
That soothes your soul's existence.

But your sensory temptations will feast,
While you travel directly into the trap of the greedy beast.

Is the title really necessary?

When titles of seniority are weak and feeble,
But titles of superficiality displayed by the youth are not
    quite quibble.

Titles of the earned chivalry and courtesy,
Do not emphasize the real prophecy.

Is the title really necessary?

If you hold on to a personal grudge,
Yet still, preach one must be their own judge?

Why then do you not practice what you preach,
And then discreetly feel for the other, the urge to impeach?

Is the title really necessary?

If wordplay is the disguise,
Just like the bold character in a play that soliloquizes.

The expectation of how they meet their end,
Keeps you at the edge of your seat, a well-known legend,

Yet hidden beneath that top layer,
Is always how the poet becomes the player.

Would you like to seek the hidden truth?
Or are you tired, and do you despise being the sleuth?

Now asks yourselves again,
Is the poem really necessary?

BACK TO THE PAST

It astonishes me,
How we so easily forget history,
As if history was not a thing of the past,
But merely something that didn't last.

What is this psychotic sycophancy?
Your obsessions with the future are, let's face it, not for
    matters of diplomacy.
It is now merely an act to dictate dictatorship,
Which clearly rules out leadership.

Long gone are the democratic ideals of liberty, equality,
    and fraternity,
You simply work on ideals of insanity.
The Republic is becoming a Leviathan,
As you are the one feeding the python.

Where is the learning in all this, the past lesson?
Or are you still going to lead us down that road of treason?
The past may have been a painful lie,
With its hushed assassinations. Oh, fie!

And with its political motives of civic unrest,
To murder till what was left were the *"purest"*.
Or its betrayal by one minister,
To overtake rule in ways that were sinister.

The past distorted the truth,
With its' erasable crimes in sleuth.
The past concealed and closeted many,
As when the door was opened, society segregated their
     company.

The past forbade ladies to shine,
Unless their beauty was used to manipulate an opine.
The past combined power with pleasure,
Irresponsible were they enough, that they also tainted
     leisure.

History was full of the unsaid,
What was written was written, but most happenings
     happened in the chamber of the bed.
The bloody battles that were fought,
The number of tyrants that were caught.

The captured land in books that were taught,
The capital estates that were bought.
The misguided emperors that practiced the opposite of
     what they preached,
The power-hungry generals that impeached.

Segregation practices or society's leech,
As ministers would propagate behaviours that beseech.
Economies thriving on aristocratic rule,
With coffers in banks, used as a tool.

Meanwhile, the past saw crime upon crime,
As poverty sent them in a rush against time.
No bread no cake could satiate the starving,
Oh, Antoinette, what were you thinking?

The Dark Ages were the darkest for the poor,
As no resource was properly stored.
War begets war,
That's what wrecked those who soared.

How can you assure yourself that we are not headed
     now in the same direction?
History repeats itself, or so is the ancient, recited
     contemplation.
And even if there were thousands of pearls under the sea,
Alas! There's now a lot that the eye cannot see.

For it has all been buried in misery,
For the past remains but a memory.
The past glories, be it of brick or of stone,
Or of marble or of an artist's ability to hone.

Ancient beauties that were explored,
Marvellous mansions built for the Lord.
The precision of ancient architecture,
With fine paintings engrained on the tombs as indenture.

The philosophies that were shared ever since the Stone
    Age,
The bright minds of the Renaissance Age,
The livelihoods of lineage that flourished,
Under dynastic rules that eventually perish.

The power that lied in the hands of the public,
For tyrants have forever feared this trick.
When freedom of speech was expressed,
On the basis of the deserving ruler, which was debated,
    not suppressed.

When rights of the Cit were widely known,
And once challenged in court, they were to hang the
    guilt-prone.
When there was a period of peace among all,
That would make a soldier stand tall.

For now, the unlocked treasures all turn rotten,
As the Future is forced to live the Forgotten.

FREEDOM

What Freedom may mean to you,
May not mean the same for me.

A puny little girl,
Who has been defeated by a bloodsucker,
Who has lost all her dignity,
Who has no longer any rights to her own body,
Will believe that *"Freedom"*, is to eliminate herself for
    good.

An innocent thief,
Who has been framed for wrongdoings,
Who has been denied justice by the authorities,
Who has been separated from his own peace of mind,
Will believe that *"Freedom"*, is to free himself from this
    vicious cycle.

A psychotic person,
Who has great difficulties in understanding the world,
Who has no sense of how to control this frustration,

Who has no sense of how to get out of this self-
    destructive locked room,
Will believe that *"Freedom"*, is to perceive life normally.

Anxious animals,
Who have been thrown into jail,
Who have become chained spirits,
Who have been agitated by strange creatures,
Will believe that *"Freedom"*, is to run around in the wild
    as free spirits.

A life protector,
Who has been there to safeguard many lives,
Who has been there to protect the borders from illegal
    infiltrators,
Who has been there to self-sacrifice in the name of the
    nation,
Will believe that *"Freedom"* is for all to live in harmony
    without the need for their service.

But,

A merciless murderer,
Who has torn a great rift in society,
Who has used the name of religion to kill,
Who has butchered many fellow beings,
Will believe that *"Freedom"* is to start up mafias of their
    own.

A righteous rapist,
Who has touched the skin of the other,
Who has tortured another,
Who has no control over their urges,
Will believe that *"Freedom"* is to play the devil without
    fear.

A corrupt conman,
Who has looted many,
Who has discreetly stabbed the backs of many,
Who has hidden wealth left unrevealed,
Will believe that *"Freedom"* is to receive as much from it
    as they can.

An illegal infiltrator,
Who has come to sell humans,
Who has come to create intentional ruckus in this nation,
Who has come to entice people to buy the drug,
Will believe that *"Freedom"* is to keep these businesses
    running.

A decisive dictator,
Who has held power for long periods of time,
Who has won votes by appealing to the innocent
    common man,
Who has played it by using the victim card,
Will believe that *"Freedom"* is to keep control over the
    masses.

A religious saint,
Who has spread intense feelings of hatred against others,
Who has ignited a fire that can't be put out,
Who has split the nation based on violence,
Will believe that "*Freedom*" is to gain more followers.

What freedom means to you,
May not mean the same for me.
For WE should not expect a change,
If THIS is what Freedom means.

THE TIME HAS COME

The time has come,
My dear one,
To step out of your comfort zone,
To raise your voice in the right tone,
To ask for a valid reason for why you must stand alone.

The time has come,
To show that every uproar,
Will be a lesson to those who soar,
Those who soar...by feeding themselves more,
While leaving the rest to ignore.

The time has come.

You ought to realize the real deceit,
Rather than focus on the past receipt,
Look at what is lurking beneath your feet,
With their conceit
...Not at what they give to you as a treat.

This is the time,

For each one of you to gain insights,
To acknowledge that your meek and feeble birth rights,
Are in the hands of these powerful dim lights,
Who leave it up to their own to cook up the bloody fights,
Who maim those who do not fit into the proportionate
     size.

There have been times of the wretched wrath,
Created to antagonize even a moth,
Where parades of undignified followers,
Turn into heartless soldiers,
With governance and humanity... sealed into a strong
     cloth.

There have been times,
Of the despicable display,
Of domination that becomes an array,
To all those who think they could play,
The game of torture with no word of say.

Times where a wheel of misfortune,

Leading by a descent into ruin,
By propagating one to be immune,
From those like a Bedouin,
Who wear scarves and caps,
Or ties and hats, or plain drapes and sacks…that do not
     practice the same tune.

And by depicting numerical figures of success,
Though tampering with numbers into excess,
Neglecting the explicit process,
So that they have access,
To build large volumes of cess.

For now, this is the time,
To dismantle and reverse every curse,
That have devalued your own self-worth,
Till you are satisfied with a purposeful verse,
To amend the bondages of those who have been dispersed.

This time is highly inevitable,

As all the harm caused to you will be curable.
To decipher their real expectations as inexplicable,
As they lead such lives that are comfortable,
While they should be held accountable,
For crimes of big and small that became fashionable.

The time
...is of the sinking truth,
Unravelled by those hidden sleuths,
So much so that their finds cause a feeling of ruth,
And a decision to join the voice of the youth!

This is the time,

To speak out on your generations of rage,
Yet remain as calm as a sage.
To notify the authorities on the worldwide stage,
That will soon cause them to cage,
All viruses that will spread in this Modern Age.

This time,
Shall compare to that of a revolution,
And just like the one of France as a conclusion,
Where the aristocracy is beheaded with absolute precision,
All die of shame till Justice becomes the head of the
    Constitution.

ON MELANCHOLIA

AN ALBATROSS LOST AT SEA

I have travelled a thousand miles,
Across Arabias, mountains and seas of time,
Witnessing the dreariness of life, while
I strolled about in the midst of the Sublime.

I, the Albatross,
Navigated through torrential downpours,
With a vision of wearing the Cross,
To follow our flawless kind from folklores.

However, my voyages of the quotidian,
Like spiritually projected journeys of a gypsy,
Destroy me from within, for I am Gideon,
I let emotions wind me up to trick me.

I've observed shells and pearls of our realm,
From my very own shell, my home.
But this Albatross, afraid, overwhelmed,
Now paralyzed to even set sail at sea, or roam.

I asked myself – "Why do I feel like Death,
Is watching my every move?
Why does my breath,
Suddenly have it's worth to prove?

Why this sudden chill down my spine?
I have previously paved the way,
For rains that prostrated me before shrines,
Why do I fear this may be my last day?"

Suddenly, a shriek howled,
As if prophesying a tempest.
A ghoul grumbled and growled,
Whilst waters around menaced.

A storm, closing in, I felt it in my claw,
All of hell, about to break loose.
I fluttered, staring at my tragic flaw,
Like staring into the eyes of a beast, preparing the noose.

My sixth sense of the storm,
Spiraling my psyche to become a drought on its way.
My vision became the prickly thorn,
...The prologue of this tragic play.

My choice, to either jump into the shallow end,
Dragging me down onto the oceanic floor.
Or to dive right into the deep bend,
To pull me close to the shore.

I chose to shut the door on Death,
Despite Death calling me out in the rain,
Inviting me to observe Oblivion lying beneath,
All those engulfed layers of pain.

My wings bore the Wrath of the Wind.
My body endured the temperature rising.
For my free spirit, strained into being pinned
...down by frightening forces, incising.

As they bore the blade of Bonaparte,
My blunt blades flapped; I was defenseless.
Strength, my only targeted dart,
As all my hope made me hopeless.

I sealed the gates on the Land of the Dead,
But had to plunge into the trenches of doom.
My sense failed me to see no land ahead,
For all I know, I was laying bricks to my tomb.

I felt trembles of thunder, a terror.
The blackness pervades,
Like fault lines, oh the horror!
Then, flashes of lightning after decades.

For it was then with a heavy heart, I decided,
To shoot down my own Albatross.
An act I shall always regret, for I, misguided,
My neck, burdened by the weight of the Cross

....and now, the body of the dead bird.
I walk with a reminder of sin on my neck.
I fall apart from within, feeling absurd.
Alas! My complete self couldn't survive the shipwreck.

I am now a soul hollowed out on the inside.
I now spend my days asking myself-

"Why?
Was it the storm that would never subside?
Or was it the anxiety caused by the sky?

Was my soul tarnished by the ravage?
Or was it affected by not being the 'ideal I'?
For the storm was not the carnage,
...I thought it was, so why?

Why did I curb my own liberation?
Was that what led me astray?
Why did my mind shut off its navigation?
Was that what made me the prey?

Was I tortured into giving up my rights?
Or was I coerced into hiding my weaknesses for so long?
Was my ambition to give up a fight?
Or did I hate death that was so prolonged?

Tell me, oh Lord! Why the silence?
Alas! I was the Mariner and the Albatross!
I can no longer stand my mind's violence.
For it was I alone who shot the Albatross!"

DROWNING IN DESPAIR

"Begone! Fie!"
Said an old lady, a passerby,
"Alas, the poor little girl is dead!"

Her sympathies,
Act as mumbled prayers under her faint breath,
As she chants in Hums of Hope.

After all,
This girl's body needs to be laid at rest,
Wherever her soul goes.

With the rotating of beads in one hand,
The elderly's eyelids suddenly droop,
To envision tranquil thoughts,

Despite Darkness drifting,
Like the Ghost of the Past,
Foregrounding their own senile existence.

All their thoughts drown in the Depths of Despair.
For humans, Death is like a thief,
Snatching away offsprings of Heaven.

So, all gather around the bodily remains,
Synchronously raising their heads high enough,
To question those Angels above.

With that, black clouds drift to hover over the scenes
    below,
A storm approaches, a thunderbolt clashes,
As waves crash onto the shore.

The body of the Dead Child, ice cold,
Rain's petrichor ruined by blood's odour,
A blood, not meant to ooze out of her.

The nature that nurtured her as a newborn,
Wept in solemn silence,
That crept and crawled in a melancholic cadence.

For her joyful memories,
Rooted in a oneness with Nature,
Now, drowned out by Despair.

High up in the skies above,
As Time mourned,
Death dreaded itself.

For taking a life not fully lived,
For it was Life that knew,
She was the epitome of vivacity.

Life and Death collapse onto each other,
As Despair renders them unconscious,
Death, now, to be tried for Negligence in court.

As the Court of Justice proceeds,
To handle the testimony,
Death's testimony...nothing but howls of grief.

Sorrow spared Death from speaking,
So Life, the Friend of Death,
Took the stand as Death's sole Defence Lawyer.

Life, with a heavy heart,
Speaks through the heart as much as the mind,
Addressing the Wise Ones of the Tribunal…

"To all the members of the jury,
Your Honour!
I wish to take the position of Defense Lawyer of the
    Accused.

I shall begin by saying the following words,
As a tribute to the troubled soul.
May she rest in peace!

The little girl, her name was Grace.
She was the most beguiling soul to ever exist,
Her persona, as pure as God.

She was all that was mystical and real,
She dreamt daily of her bonds with nature,
Oh! What a beauty she was!

As if playing a part in a true fairytale,
She chased after Dandelions,
She childishly imitated the roars of Lions.

She sparkled like the dew of a rose,
She awakened even the Dawn,
She glided with the Dove that soars,

She galloped with the Horses,
She dived with the Dolphins,
All so, with a gullible giggle.

Her playtime with the dolls,
All reminded us of a glass menagerie,
As the clearest Art as her heart of hearts.

Her happiness indeed made us smile,
Her sadness moved our kind to tears,
Nevertheless, she was in her Innocence.

Alas, Fate's prudish knowledge,
Decided to drown her out with Death,
For Fate works in mysterious ways.

Death may have not known this,
But I, as Life, witnessed her,
And her fatal flaw, firsthand.

Persuaded by the touch of Toxicity,
Surveilled by the claw of Control,
Blinded by the Senses of Shade,

Ignited by an inner Animosity,
She dared to challenge Curiosity,
To let her visualize vehement Youth.

Only to her realisation that,
Like a prophecy, this forbidden knowledge,
Would lead her to her own doom.

For Youth wasn't all that it seemed it was,
Rage, accompanied by the blade or bullet,
And Fear, with the pellet.

Freedom was a word beating its own back,
As the girl stared right into states of lawlessness,
Her imagination, killed on sight, till it spiralled.

Curiosity, bound by the Law of Time,
And the Principles of the Mind,
Had no option but to offer Grace, visions of Life's journey.

Oh, Curiosity!
My sympathies lie with you,
For I know your heart lies with Innocence...and always
    will.

If only the Ways of the World,
Had granted you your rights,
To act like a shield from the Real Realm,

You wouldn't fall prey to all predators around,
Who feed on feeble brains,
Till they become marionettes tied to strings.

Having lost all that ardour,
Till they achieve solely languor,
In the presence of the Beast.

Alas! For you, fiction wasn't even an option.
As stated by the Testament of Truth,
"Thou shalt speak, but the Truth."

Your Honour!
As I bear witness to her Life and Death,
I can say that even Grace's Sight wept,

As Innocence, instantly snatched,
Away from under her feet,
Like pulling away sheets of her bed, as she sleeps.

God's grace was replaced by Grace's Despair,
Even as she elegantly smiled through her agony,
It was her spirit that was wounded by another's vanity.

She kept her poised self for the Superior others,
But deep inside, she was a wreckage weeping, corroded,
Her poise injected with poison.

The images she envisioned,
Haunted her in her own mirror,
She despised Horror peering at her door.

Dearest Death,
Despair not!
Visualisation was her Death.

No matter how much I attempted to reduce her anxieties,
She would fall more into the pits of Despair,
And let the sinkhole consume her being.

Slight mutters heard in Court

Begone! Fie!
Innocence, the culprit?
Oh Judicious Jury, kindly humble them into using
    words wisely.

Oh, Innocence! Oh, sweet Innocence!
You were the victim as much as Curiosity,
I can only pray for your recovery.

Your Honour,
At first, all our forces had followed the Plan of Protocol,
Setting the conflict and the resolution.

Innocence put up a fight,
Like one I've never seen before,
Unfortunately, the resolution, Innocence had to surrender,

Resisting Innocence was trampled over,
By the Herculean forces of Youth,
I, the Observer witnessed forces form Life's Resolution.

The War of Age came to an end,
With Youth emerging as Victorious,
Prideful Youth finally was to come of Age.

The Law of Order states that-

"The Oracle of Youth,
Must be handed over once Maturity
Becomes triumphant in battle.

The Scroll of Life must be passed on
From Youth tête-à-tête to the recipient,
In the same fashion as mentioned with Innocence."

Sadly, even Youth turned a blind eye to Grace's plight,
Unaware of the unnatural phenomena,
Of Grace carrying this Oracle even before her Time.

Grace, overshadowed by the Shady forces,
Of Fate, foresaw what was to come,
Thus, breaking Nature's desired course of Time.

Youth was deceived just when it was received,
Alas! Grace was born with a curse,
Now our entire family is crumbling into pieces.

So let us rise above this call for revenge,
As well as pity for each other,
For the Order is all falling apart.

Grace, oh how we all loved her!
How we all admired her for her charm!
How we all made merry the time she finally spoke her
    mind with calm!

Sadly, Grace's Fate was Death either way,
It was Darkness that led her astray.
May her blessed soul rest in peace!

Oh, the Horror!
The doll she so adored in childhood,
Was to be tainted and tarnished.

Oh, the Horror!
This glass figurine we all imagined her to be,
Was oozing out with blood not meant to ooze out of her.

It was only when she wept wildly in remorse,
Lamenting her being easily swayed by the Winds of Fate,
To read her Chronicle of a Death Foretold.

Whilst pondering on what could have been,
I witnessed her lay there, irresolute and still,
As she bemoaned the bloody betrayal.

That was when Death answered her.
The uncanny timeliness of this event,
Can only be answered by Fate itself.

Your Honour,
It was Death who comforted her,
Welcoming her with the doors wide open.

The traumas that haunted Grace,
God rest her soul!
But it is time we let her go!

It is time... to rewrite the Constitutions of Existence."

IN THE MEADOWS OF A SHADOW

A shadow stretched till far in shades of grey,
The landscape's tendency forgives the opine,
One ignores this light of day,
While one surpasses the tides of the sublime.

Let it hover over your head,
Let it cover the very sheets of your bed,
Let it bother your mind for what has been said,
Let it discover the one who has always led.

Your heart that hurts in pain,
Your mind that punishes,
Your little self, though in vain,
Your soul in wanton desire for refurbishes.

Within the demarcations of a shadow,
That this gloomy footpath tread,
You subconsciously discover the ground a'hallow,
Will have some relief, as sworn by this oath as read.

You are led to a marshy meadow,
The Surroundings make your eyes fickle,

Serenity touches where all seems mellow,
While you stroll around and your thoughts heckle.

In these meadows of a shadow,
Let your soul dance in this dullness of wonderment,
Let your being sing to the melodies of this episodic
    enchantment,
Let your body bathe and tan in this merriment.

In the meadows of a shadow,
Dwell not on the intense insights,
But on living among the colourful lights,
Think not from a place of reality,
But in the mind envisioning purity.

Fill the hole till the whole of your heart,
Is drenching in this anointed glow,
The mind takes you to fantastical places, an
    appreciative art,
While you imagine nature as to how winds blow.

Guide yourself to this meadow in the shadow once in a
    while.

LITTLE BOY

Little boy,

Speak your mind,
Speak your heart,
Speak from the very depths of your soul.

Little boy,

Your soul was sent,
To experience the unconditional parental love,
So feel it, embrace it, express it, let it quench the very
thirst of your soul.

Little boy,

Smile a little longer,
Laugh a little louder,
For your soul will feel true happiness,
In times of desolate sadness.

Little boy,

Your time will be up,
Just when you are about to crawl,
For that was God's will,
For your strength will always be your pure,
        unadulterated smile.

Little boy,

Fulfill your destiny,
And achieve glory that will last till eternity,
For you will teach your own how to fully live,
And you will teach all how to fight till there is no more
        reason left to fight.

Little boy,

You have nothing to hide,
So give it all you have got,
Fight till your last breath,
Knowing that this is one struggle you will not face in
        your next life.

Little boy,

Dream of a world full of fantasy,
Treat everything you lay your hands upon as a mystery,
For your curiosity will teach you whatever you must
        learn in this life,

You will be enchanted by complexions,
You will be mesmerized by elements of surprise.

Little boy,

Feel the pain in your heart,
Though you must never forget who you really are,
And to whom you will return,
For He is the one who will truly heal your heart,
And your soul.

Little boy,

Sing and dance joyously,
As this time,
You will give your parents the pleasure of having a first
    child,
Tears of felicity will soon turn to tears of sorrow,
Alas! You will not live to face the tomorrow.

Little boy,
Your forever will always be those familiarised faces,
So though you will miss their love,
You will regain all that you have lost and more,

In the next life.

Despair not, my sweet little boy,
Rest in the arms of God,
Till we meet again…

MOMENTS AWAY FROM THE SHADOWS

Moments away from the shadows,

I chant prayers,
And sing lullabies to myself once in a while,
To cease my moods from being corrupted.

Moments away from the shadows,

I hum the tunes of my ancestors when I feel hostile,
Who reminds me of my roots,
That have since ages been constructed.

Moments away from the shadows,

I follow the steps of my kin,
That trace back to the settlements around the river Nile,
I dance in the name of the Lord who strengthens my
    memory that choreographed.

Moments away from the shadows,

I write calligraphic poems,
And stories of today that seem worthwhile,
Which are truths that cannot be disputed.

Moments away from the shadows,

I paint and wash away any sins and troubles,
With watercolours that form my portfolio profile,
I hold my paintbrush in my right hand with a palette
        that seems diluted.

Moments away from the shadows,

I recite the words of the Prophet, Jesus, Moses, and The
        Buddha.
Till my heart, in beguile,
Historically, perplexities of the conscience of our kind
        were pricked by the bigoted.

And therefore,

Moments away from the shadows,
I hum, I sing, I chant, I dance, I recite, I write, I paint,
Though, not in pain...

TO DEAREST GOD PART 1

To Dearest God,

Oh Dear Lord,
Mustn't you show mercy on those,
Who have blinded us with hatred.

Oh Dear Lord,
Mustn't you shower blessings on those,
Who have made us grief-stricken.

Oh Dear Lord,
Mustn't you allow survival of those,
Who have doomed us with their enticing words.

Instead, show your love to those who are not like them.
Instead, allow those innocents to stand up 'gainst all evil.
Instead, lead the way to peaceful coexistence.

Yours truly,
One of your creations

As this letter was sent to heaven,
By those angelic, yet mysterious beings,
The Almighty summoned Death to pick up this fellow
    being from this world.

As the soul detached from the body,
The soul reaches her final destination,
Called *"Paradise"* as humans put it.

The Supreme soul, whom all worshipped stands right in
    front of her-

Oh, Dear Child,
I received your letter from your guardian angels.

Oh, Dear Child,

'Tis I who have formed this world out of my free will,
'Tis I who have the power to give and take away,
'Tis I who have the right to charge one of treason.

'Tis I whom you seek everywhere,
'Tis I whom you fight about,
'Tis I who foresees tragic and horrific events, but
    changes none.

But, oh my poor child,

'Tis not I who you must blame,
'Tis not I who is responsible for your actions,
'Tis not I who can help mend what you have already
    broken.

For you all must be held accountable,
for every devilish act you commit,
For you have divided your own kind,
For you have planted all roots of evil, not I,
For you trick others to fall into your own trap.

Though *you* might be innocent,
If I was to destroy all evil,
You wouldn't know how the face of evil looks like,
You wouldn't be able to bear any evil,
You wouldn't be able to end any evil.

After all, oh dear child,
'My duty' is to guide and teach you,
'Your duty' is to reach the finish line on your own.

Dearest child,

I free you from your wrongdoings in your past life,
After all, your vile actions are the reason for your present
    sufferings.
And the ones who previously suffered terribly,
Are reincarnated as the *'misfits'* of today.
Hence, I see you all as one.

There will be an end to this world very soon,
There will be a shortage,
There will be a rebellion.

It may take many human years,
It may mean you are forced to walk miles in a deserted
     land,
It may take you on a spiritual journey leading to
     exhaustion.

It will take willpower, not just strength from your side,
It will take more than just truth and honesty,
It will make you realize the power that love holds in this
     universe

…as it lightens up this dark world,
To get to what you call, *"Peace on Earth"*.

But dear child, don't lose hope.
Remember-
For I will always be there with you,
For I love all of you equally,
For I will always guide you to your desired destination.

Yours forever
and always,
God

After this trip to paradise,
The soul returned in yet another form,
As a saviour,
As fearless and brave,
As loving and affectionate,
As God told her to be.

TO DEAREST GOD PART II

"Oh Dear Lord,

Why must I treat my mind as my worst enemy?
Why must I dream of death?
Why must I seem so desperate to be heard by you?

Why do I live in fear?
Why do I feel like I need to dig deeper?
Why do I have intense emotions of despair?

Why shall my mind tell me to hurt myself in the most
    inhumane ways?
Why shall I turn to my devils to hide the truth?
Why shall I seek revenge?"

While hearing these depressing thoughts of one fellow
    being,
The Almighty one chooses to express themself
By answering through a letter-

Oh, Dear Child,

You must remember-
I created You with a purpose,
I save You with a dignity,
I gently explain every road You take through dreams,
I send soulful mortals into Your life to guide You,
I leave behind a message in every thought of Yours,

Why think of your mind as your worst enemy?

Instead,

Treat your mind as an acquaintance accompanying you
    on life's journey.
When your mind starts to bully you,
You have the courage to resist that toxicity,
And bring peace to your mind.
Forgive yourself for mistakes of the past and present,
Yet take responsibility to bring it all back to balance.

I must tell you-
What works best is if instead of *searching* for a God,
Know and *believe* there is a God.

Rejuvenate every cell of your body,
By basking in the sun and the shadows.
Why think of your mind as your worst enemy?
Rather, must you see it that way,
You will destroy whatever You Had,
You Have, and whatever You Will Have.

You will bring to an end, your hard-earned soul,
As the soul, you have in this life,
Has gone through continuous cycles
…of regeneration to reach this current body of yours.
Your soul knows its purpose and its worth.
Now it is time for your 'being' to decipher theirs.

Your very psyche reflects you dreaming of Death.
My initial intention was to instill thoughts into
    humankind,
As merely a method of experimentation and exploration,
To see you curious mortals try and test hypotheses.
But now, you mortals question the existence of me,
And my very own acquaintance, Death.

Now you all believe that it is a hoax.

Our Existence is unimportant now that Science is by
    your side.
As you have taken it upon yourselves to play God anyhow.
Now, one doesn't even need Death to summon them,
One can simply discard every reason to live,
And inflict terror, havoc, harm, and violence,
To destroy everything we spirits stand for, are you
    humans happy now?

For I now see that Death has not been able to fulfil its
    duty,
And lies vacant…waiting…waiting

…Waiting for those who are loyal to Death to give a
    signal,
While you are blind to all but darkness,
Your soul very well knows it chose this body of yours,
To experience emotions that you call *unbearable*.

You convince yourself that you are being *tortured* by
    your heart,
But you all forget that to live is to feel.
If you hadn't muted your own feelings,
And shut your eyes to the heart that beholds the true You,
All so that you could cope with reality,
Your life wouldn't be as difficult as it seems.

Are you aware of all that surrounds you?
Are you really that grateful for the water you drink, the
    food you eat?
Your prayers, do they mean anything to you?

Your thoughts are listened to.
Your heart beats as One.
You meet like-minds who embrace you in your weakest
    moments,
I drive you to break free from all that troubles you too,
The energies sent by the Universe warn you of the
    darkness.
So why need you be desperate to be heard in a world
    that clearly doesn't?

For living in fear, is that entirely true?

Is it the fear of not being seen and heard or the fear of
    Life?
Is it the fear of commitment or the fear of feeling
    unaccomplished?
Is it the fear of losing a loved one or the fear of seeing
    death?
For you mortals are wired with fear as a survival
    instinct,
It is natural to live with fear, like prey fearing for their life,
Although your inner self determines the meaning of fear
    for itself.

Introspection is the key to enhancing the depth of
    perception.
Let Life's flow take you on a mystical voyage,
Enlightening you to envision the truth that lay right
    before you.
One day, you shall see yourself for who You truly are.
You shall observe worlds that go beyond your very own.
So, you must dig deeper, you must…dig deeper.

What is Hope and Despair?

On the one hand, neglecting shadows to see light is
    what you call 'hope'.
On the other, hiding inside the shadows is what you call
    'despair'.

Thereby, the equilibrium of energies is tipped,
Leading you to experience extremities in emotions,
For you must see the shadows yet still see the light,
To broaden your horizons in life, like a zoom-out lens.

How dare you seek and plot revenge as if it is yours to
     give?

You ought not to blind yourself with hatred,
For I have seen a tragic loss in humanity,
As lost souls lose directions, for them, all hope is lost.
So, they take it upon themselves to restore justice.
Must You not act in such ways, for You are not like
     them,
It is I who must deal with them, not You.

You shall be saved with dignity yet again.

You seem to not remember what is clearly known to
     you,
I must remind you that You are Unique.
Your incandescent strife is what uplifts You.
Your joyful sorrow is what empowers You.
You are not simply what defines You.
So why must you suppress the pain? Embrace it.

For You are The Approachable One,
Your curious carelessness is what inspires others,

Your painful passion is what others protect from You.
Rest your faith in me.

I assure you the Universe will align for You.
For your true partner is your Omniscient Soul.

Blessing you always,
God

As God writes this letter,
They feel so overwhelmed,
So, they extract some of their elixirs,
And donates it to another immortal soul,
To their loved acquaintance, Death.

DEATH SPEAKS FOR ITSELF

Death enters the light,
And looks at an acquaintance, God, in the shadows.
Death turns to God,
And God faces Death.
The eyes of God,
Meet Death.
And Death,
Meets the eyes of God.

God and Death both acknowledge each other and bid
farewell.
For God's being evaporates,
From the haze combined with the shadows.
Behind God's evaporating body,
A little boy emerges as if by hallucination.
Death sees the little boy and is reminded of its' youth.
For Death notices from far a saline teardrop,
Ready to fall on this pure land.

Death approaches this little boy,
As a motherly instinct,
In a fatherly fashion,

For in that one moment,
A connection was built between Death and the boy.
As the figure of Death reached the boy,
The little boy broke into a burst full of tears.
A tear after tear after tear fell.

For Death couldn't help but ask the little boy-
"Dear son,
What brings you here?
For your teardrops make my heart ache.
Speak oh child speak!"
The little boy,
Chokes up his sobs, and feebly speaks
…of how he wants to rob himself of his own life.

Death replies-

"Oh, child,
Death may seem soothing,
As it is your souls' comfort zone.
It is your original place of home,
Where you spend your entire life in death.

Death may seem pleasant,
As there is a shift from the insane to sane.
Your soul is laid to rest,
And lies under my protection.
Your thoughts no longer taunt, trouble, and disturb.
Your visions are no longer tampered with.

Your heart no longer becomes hardened.
For once you reach me, there is nothing but silence.

Death may seem courageous and bold,
As there is a battle one has to fight
…to die while you live.
Emotions eat you up inside and feed into your soul.
The war that never ends,
Until the living body evaporates,
And disintegrates into atoms and molecules,
Post a being's death which further generates new forms
    of life.

Death may seem like indulging in bliss,
As there are no expectations held after death.
For you can turn to the true version
…of your own self.
Your soul is neither expecting nor pleading for attention.
Your soul is humbly aware of God's affections,
As well as my caring intentions.
For gratitude lies in your acceptance.

Death…
…may seem irresistible.
For the assorted flavours of compassion,
Just like the temptation of promiscuity in life.
Though souls only attract unadulterated partners.
For the souls attract one another,

The process may seem obscure,
Though the combinations are universally secure.

Oh, Little One!

What is the point of calling upon Death?
Death is given to all as a reward for challenging and
    facing life.
Life may be a tragic farce,
But death is nothing but a place of utopia.
What is your soul without Life?
Moreover, what is Death without Life?
Death is for those who have earned me
…not for those who covetously dwell about me.

There is indeed life
…after a new death.
But sadly, there is also death
…after a new life.
Deaths happen in life too.
They may seem tragic,
Where all individuals tremor,
At the sight of their fortune teller.

But unlike the fortune-tellers who predict your life on
    the basis of moving celestial bodies,

These inner fortune tellers,
Predict your dark side,
Depict your dilemma as bonafide,
Contradict your morals if you hide,
Addict you to the conception of suicide.
Child, know that the pangs of life are different from the
	pangs of death.
The truth is that souls can never attain a proper life in
	death
…if they die in life.

So, leave it to God and I to protect you.

For Gratitude is soothing.
Resilience is bold.
Convalescence is irresistible.
For knowing your life's purpose is utter bliss.
For using your conscience is why you chose life in the
	first place.
Little boy, the hardest part of life is confronting dangers
	and death,
And the hardest part after death is living only one side
	of life.
So then why choose Death over Life?"

The little boy
…who prior to this sudden insight,
Was standing up on a chair,

Mourning for his life,
Took the advice of Death,
To forgive himself for dying in life,
While he had a chance of living,
As he gave himself a second chance to come out alive.

THE WAY OF WORDS

CLIO

AN ODE TO A LOVER

This is an ode to a lover-

"The first time I met you,
Till the last time, I will see you,
There will forever remain one thing constant,
In this forever-changing universe,
And that is my love…. for you."

This is what we hear from one lover to another,
Just like the other to another lover.

For this is a sham,
And a scandalous scam.
You let one hurt till they have been damned,
And consider it was love from this other man.
And here I present to you my ode to the lover-

Dear lovers of this great world,

Do you even know what Love is?
Are you aware of its sentiment or merely its testament?
Is Love expressible or is Love the very expression?

Why do you say you have fallen in love?
Rather than rising and growing in love?

Fallen is just like that angel who had fallen,
For having obsessions over his own demeanour,
Fallen is just like bearing a wound after you have…
     fallen onto the ground,
Fallen is just like a desperation to let go of your own self,
And drown it in the depths of the sea,

Where all the blood that flows from the arteries to the
vein and then the vein to the arteries,
Just drifts from the body of a lover,
As this torture made him dream of how he should be
     falling.
Fallen is like the drops of dew that have fallen from a
     leaf in the midst of the fog,
Just like teardrops that have fallen in the midst of the
     hazy atmosphere,

Fallen is just like a parasitic syndrome,
That leeches onto your back,
While you anxiously wait for their track,
But they go out to find more to sack,
Till you have fallen…

So, is love for the fallen?

To the lovers,
Who choose to type a message,
Rather than meet through a passage.
The fear of communication is indeed like concubinage,
For your texts reveal a cleavage.

To the lovers,
Who hug and open the other up.
Who touch and kiss but still seem to miss...the emotion.
As they hug and open another up,
And touch and kiss but still seem to miss.... the point.

To the lovers,

Who are 'sick' of building up the stamina,
Why don't you try telling that to her vagina?
Who are in denial of damaging the elegant ballerina,
While she could have just flaunted herself as a charming
    signorina,
She, the antonym of signorina, whilst having given birth
    to another in these established cognomina.

To the lovers,
Who like spies against criminals, hover over the other,
In an attempt to not disconnect from the other,
But are not content with the friendly affection they
    smother,
And choose to dominate the feelings till that someone is
    left bothered.

To the lovers,
Who hurt and intentionally flirt,
Who likes picking up the dirt,
Who likes going to some other to blurt,
Let me just start by saying- you know nothing of Love!

So don't you dare go saying-
"The first time I met you,
Till the last time, I will see you,
There will forever remain one thing constant,
In this forever changing universe, and that is my love.... for
        you."

Don't you dare go on by saying-
"I will never leave you."
Don't you dare go on by saying-
"I want to make love to you."
DON'T YOU DARE SAY – *"I love you"*.

Love is no message on text,
Or chapter in a book.
Love if not cherished,
Can turn blank even till the next,
Time you go and peek a look.

Love is no melody,
No rhythm,
No symphony,

No synonym.
If you cannot love the other with your full heart.

Cause love doesn't just mean,
Those butterflies,
Those irregular heartbeats,
That grieving demise,
Those intense flushes of heat.

Love is not as symbolic as a rose.
Love is not just some Petrarchan prose.
Love just doesn't require any such talent shows.
Love is not necessarily a rich persons' please.
Love is not a spread of disease.

Now when we hear the term *"rising in love"*, it says it all.
One goes through the darkest of times,
But will be supported by the other just like a gardener to
    a flower.
Just like these simplified rhymes,
They share a symbiotic relationship that empowers.

Love,
Is that one sad moment,
That lets you feel the emotion.
Yet ensures you don't dwell in that melancholic scent,
And allows you to vent out all that confusion.

Love,

Is the knowledge.

For you don't have to say those three words,

For the love connection starts with the act of
    acknowledging,

Which later grows into a song of the hummingbirds.

Love,

Is the belief,

That permits you both to live life on your own accord,

Yet also guides you just like a parental figure when you
    are accompanied by mischief.

And makes sure you can afford…a fort for your own self.

For love is the desire,

To want the best for your partner,

To not complain when they have accomplished more
than what you do.

For as much as I have understood,

"Love is much bigger than us all."

This is my ode to the lovers.

A TRAIN OF THOUGHT

The thought stationed at rest,
Begins its' journey,
From one word to another.
The destinations await,
Connecting the lengths and breadths,
Of the nexus of nations,
…to make meaning.

The farewell cries,
Seen as the train departs.
Wailing words who will miss their collectives,
As a training program of community service commences.
These letters know their purpose,
To deliver a message,
To their receiver.

Alas! These soldiers of strength,
Will tragically trespass territories,
Only to die on the battlefield.

On board, the thoughtful train also collects,
Prejudiced passengers,

Stereotypical snitches,
The disturbed and downtrodden,
And complex cerebral commuters,
The train also trains the travellers,
To build their diplomatic connections.

These connections are vital,
To unjumble the jumbled.
Where the jargon juxtaposes,
The proper phrase procedure.
The train conductor named Eerie Editing,
Compartmentalizes conjunctions,
And finally, interrogates interrogations.

The thought now enters a dark tunnel,
Where the futile find their freedom,
To terrorize the texts to commit thievery,
Incomprehensible inventions become indestructible.
The dispute destroys indifferences,
The sorted start squealing and spiralling.
The quest becomes quite queer with no erratic errors
    erased.

Clashes confuse collaboration with corrosion,
The significant strive for simple safety,
Whereas the deathly "DO NOT'S"
…dreadfully dream of dominance.
War wages wreckages.

All this blackness
…burns and bleeds.

When now this train exits the tunnel,
With a little luminescence,
Though thoughts become besmeared,
With such sinful thinking-
That there is no more of that wishful thinking.
The train, delayed,
Must reach its' destination.

So, it rapidly races
To reach the subsequent stops.
The conductor commands the commas
To sacrifice themselves
for the excessive weight of the train
Extinguishing thoughts
Are forced into overdrive

Seated signals now become a stained spark as they slay
     with their sword
Though descent diverts the directed course.
This dissent also decides to drive the dissemination
The train tracks that are laid out no more
While the railway rashly and rapidly accelerates
Over the hills of hope, to the terrains of terror
Into the fiery forests of fury

The train almost clashes and collides
Tons of thousands of resourceful recruits
Lose their lives and loves
Jeopardy juggernauts…

The mighty battle fought on tracks
From within, arises a saintly saviour
The pen plays the part of Perseus
Who slays slithering sermons
And morbidly, monstrous marks

The pen emerges in enlightenment
Knowledgeable and intelligible
to radiate resolution
In an attempt to arouse an alliance.

"An armistice accordingly that is to appease,
Both behaviours of bereavement.
Cadence must condemn the corruptive contempt.
Discretion must delete diabolical diminution.
Eradication of enterprise must be enumerated.
Fundamental foundations should free the fountainhead
… Zephyrs of zeal now must be the new normalcy."

Such are the clauses of this contract,
Written in calligraphic calibrations,
That are meticulously maintained,
To call for a ceasefire.

The train, bloody as it is,
Cleanses compartments, cabinets, and coaches.
Meanwhile, the mighty pen marauders the murderers,
Till *"the guilty"* gear themselves up for the guillotine.

And so,
the restoration remains dignified.
The remaining soldiers seek asylum,
For their survival at the cost of their sanity.

These words now wail with a weak whisper.
The quill quaintly quivers and cries.
These phrases put together,
on a parchment of paper
…Form a powerful poem

…that transforms thoughts,
into terrified tones of recital.
The writhing writings repeated,
till one is lost for words.

A train full of thoughts,
Screeched to a stop.
With a drop that stains in pain.
The pen plays like a piper,
With melodies of melancholia,
Till tears from sullen faces
…run down in memorabilia.

'Tis a story one shall tell,
Till Time beguiles the new dawn,
As all are aroused into immediate action,
Respite resurrects and resurges

…into eternal radiance,
That shall turn the dials of time.
A train of thoughts…
…now… immortalized in ink.

THROUGH THE LABYRINTH OF INDECISION

When the fog blurs not only your eyesight,
But your mind, heart, and soul,
When the clouds overwhelm you,
To shed tears, like the sordid rain.

When you are unable to decipher,
Whether Resilience has your back,
Or if to shrink back into your shell
…Shell Of Ignorance.

That is when ventilation,
Becomes the need of the hour.
Though your room has no such escape,
As the haze sets in, clouding your judgements.

Polarizing as the magnetic forces are,
The room is now divided into two halves,
As you linger, shifting between the two,
Like the lost souls residing in Dante's limbo.

With a firm step forward,
And two steps backward.
You try to cross the paths ahead,
Then, realize the positioning of the mirror.

The mirror, placed in the centre,
Becomes your tracking piece,
Tracing each step synchronously,
Simultaneously, showing your truth.

So, you streamline your figure,
To balance yourself on the beam ahead,
You swiftly make it midway,
To head towards the focal point.

At this moment,
Your strategy is as clear and calm,
As smart and manipulative,
As one who has mastered the game of chess.

Though, you soon come to realize,
That the frame is rusting,
The glass is cracking,
And the image is distorting.

The unconducive atmosphere of air,
Permeates, only to settle as dust particles.
Until you suffer from shallow breaths,
And silently die inside.

The pollution becomes a part of your life,
Until you part with life,
For the defense mechanism used-
Rationalisation, to avoid the protective mask.

Your hope is to come to a conclusion,
In this game played on your life.
For you give way to your own arrogance,
And decide you won't take time.

You choose to drown in the deep dark realm,
Of your own thoughts,
While inhaling the smog,
Rather than steer clear from Death itself.

Seek peace or no peace with it,
It will always seem to drag you down,
For it also dwells in your dreams,
Even if you pretend to seek peace.

Paralysis, as a result.
Immobility forces you to kneel before Fate,
Riot and mutiny spurt into disorder,
As all hell breaks loose.

As if the room is possessed by a ghost,
The room suddenly locks itself,
As you succumb to your insecurities,
Room bound with your anxieties.

You yell, shout, scream, cry,
You plead, you please.
To escape the groans and creaks,
Or the shrieks of your own ghouls.

The pea soup fog of the room,
Transforms it into the haunted forests,
During the Devil's hour.
It terrifies you; it petrifies you.

The guiding lights, nowhere to be found,
Darkness, a fuel added to the fire,
As despair disrupts and dystopian lands erupt,
This foul air weighs down on the Weak.

The room now becomes your gas chamber,
You suffocate in the same room,
As your long-lost ancestors,
Or depressed tenants, with a different cause.

Until you hear a melodic sound,
A place of momentary happiness,
This permits you to take a breath,
Amidst what is unbreathable.

That is when you receive Divine Intervention.
As your closed eyelids envision the light,
The glow grows in you,
The shine sparks positivity in you.

The light becomes your immunity,
As each cell, each organ,
Senses the need to fight back,
The virus eventually reduces to nothing.

Like a wiped windshield,
You finally start to think clearly.
So, you grab the mask.
Ridding yourself of all toxicity first.

You follow the safety protocol sheet,
To survive the surrounding low oxygen,
Similar to that of a plane,
For you know you still have to face the storm.

In search of your very own key,
You walk for what feels like miles in a desert,
Each tap, each move felt by you,
Till your heart beats the closer you come to it.

You blindly follow the Light within,
Amongst the Darkness that invades you.
Further, your familiarity of the divided spaces,
Is what becomes your compass.

As and when you step into an unfamiliar zone,
You notice there is much left to hone,
So, you use your touch sensation,
To feel each corner left in this place.

You stumble across an object that ticks,
You stumble over another that pricks,
You fall flat on a few foundational bricks,
And walk past the magician playing tricks.

Though, you show full faith and courage,
As you charge ahead in one direction.
The noises of your mind now silenced,
As you suddenly hear the clink of the key.

As you reach for the key below your feet,
Your heightened sense of touch,
Leaves you in awe,
The purity of the metal used shocks you.

This untainted key of Knowledge,
Becomes one of your very own treasure chests.
So, you make your way back,
Through the labyrinth.

You walk towards the familiarized door,
Travel those conquered lands yet again.
Walk across to the first half of the room.
And open the lock to the Gates of Wisdom.

Sight itself becomes your sword,
As you fight time with your well-gained agility.
And as you reach your destination,
The mask or your shield is finally taken off.

You soon realize, it was wisdom which came,
From not guidance, but experience.
You put yourself through the Ultimate Test,
By risking it all, by fighting it all.

Till you finally found what you were seeking,
You found your Answer, your Calling.

CALL OUT YOUR MUSE

The blind breathe the shades of the soul,
The mute speaks of otherworldly words till recited in a
    scroll.

The bleakness of the shadow,
Become the mournful mellow.

The isles of isolation,
Heighten the hallucination.

The philosophies of the Cosmos,
Unknown, undiscovered, playing in pianissimos.

Despair not!

For sorrow is silenced by a space,
An energy lifts you to travel to some place.

However, Hypnosis hides your Muse,
Until you call out that name, as you choose.

You focus your heart in your head,
And choose to commemorate the dead.

Your memories, a clear channel,
For you follow footsteps, filtering like a funnel.

You are beckoned by The Calling,
Songs and sonnets of the heart, a-soaring.

The Lyre and The Muse awaken,
To enliven earthly senses once forsaken.

You find solace in grace,
And happiness, that you entirely embrace.

You find a history of beauty,
As deciphering becomes your duty.

The Divine will draw a delicate dream.
The Almighty will act in a silent scene.

While the Protector, Guide, and Preserver,
Obligate themselves as your own Observer.

The Universe is what shall understand,
As you learn to unravel the unplanned.

You symbolize metaphors and rhythms,
Heartbeats become instrumental anthems.

The vibrance of reverberations,
Chromatize crescendo vibrations.

The chaos of colour,
Known well to the passionate practitioner.

Colour upon colour meets the closéd eye,
Its fluorescence is what fires the firefly.

Perceptive glances and distortions,
Fiddle with figurative interpretations.

Whilst the hum becomes a chant,
An orchestral organ becomes a confidante.

Though the black background,
Begins to harmonize a serendipitous sound.

Fade into the night,
But then, return to the depths of the light.

Gorge your saintly senses,
In the plenty purified presences.

For that is when you shall find your own sound,
In the midst of the Marvellous, so profound.

Your voice, now independent,
That roars and rises like a Revenant.

Alas!
Short-lived, you slip back into a slumber,
Like a newborn babe with countless curiosities you
    encounter.

The rabbit who returns to its hole,
For that is the legend you have been told.

Magic is what pulls a rabbit out of the hat,
Like a rabbit, your muse, in a hidden habitat.

You attempt your hand in the arts that are,
What leads you to the stars.

Your tonal quality zoned out,
Though, fragrant finesse is what is found out.

Continue on the pious path to peruse,
And you shall meet your Muse.

Oh, Magnificent Maxime,
Innovate the illustrious unforeseen!

ODE TO THE WRITTEN WORD

To all those prose writers who think they know a thing
or two about what it is to be a poet, they think they
have the gall,
To all those despotic poets that decide their works
should be framed to achieve immortality,
To all those competitive thinkers who secretly know
their productions are only to prove they are the
know-it-all,
To all those Petrarchan lovers who pen down their
emotions to gain a sense of passing the blame which
feels satisfactory,

To all those depressing yet still confessing individuals
who get away with writing a thing or two about
suffering,
To all those "philosophical" poetic players who
plagiarize,
To all those demented playwrights who experience
artistic buffering,
To all those poems that are dedicated to that one person
in their life to apologize.

HOW CAN YOU BE SO SELFISH?
That in writing in the structure of a prose,
You talk only about how you are the fish,
Caught in that bowl about which everyone knows.

You talk about your miseries,
Your displeasing memories,
Your frustration, your insight.
Your contemplation, your stand for the right.

You talk about the visions that you carry forward,
No, that holds you back.
You talk about the moments you got that reward,
No, but they didn't cut you some slack.

You talk about your personal experience,
In the meantime, you portray your relationships as toxic.
You are the victim with a loose conscience,
While your problems are *"larger than life"* as these
    experiences have made you dyslexic,

And then you say you are socially aware?
HOW DARE YOU!
Because this Greta Thunburgian idea was not something
    that just came out of thin air!
HOW DARE YOU!

Your wounds are that of petty scars and bruises, so
    HOW DARE YOU glorify victimhood,
Through the mere use of poetry!
Have you really ever understood,
What it truly means to write a poem, with the
    appropriate use of simile?

Your poetic knowledge restricted to a fraction of a one-
    fifth,
While the exploration till its very roots is vast and deep.
There is more to a night than just the twelfth,
So let that sink in while you think about it in your sleep.

HOW DARE YOU!

You have the audacity to strike a pose,
And call that a poem.
For all that I care, you might as well just win that talent
    show,
Though know that you are performing your own requiem.

HOW DARE YOU!

Now since you like to feed on that little ego of yours,
Let's just say- you don't deserve even a metre of poetry!
For poetry has a lot more to it than just pitying yourself
    over past sores,
You really don't deserve even the sight of poetry.

Poetry is too complex,
Too easy to perplex,
It's an art that not many can master,
While playing their part.

Poetry is MORE than an art,
It is innate to every human being,
The trees of knowledge that a poem can impart,
Is more than their grandmother, their mother, and they
    will ever be seeking!

Poetry doesn't need titles of appreciation,
Or awards of felicitation.
Poetry is the sole purpose for all there is in a human
    form of life,
Poetry is that all in one just like that of a wife.

The power of the poem recitations,
Contrary to science, is nothing compared to energy
    produced by light.
It has universal dynamics which allows for sonic
    reverberations,
Words akin to ballet resonate to soothe the night.

The mind, body, and soul at peace,
Rhythmic beats harmonious with the pleasant visuals.
For all other senses that exist, cease.
It is a presence so spiritual.

To be able to feel that sense of connect,
Is otherworldly.
For once we realize there is more to protect,
Poetry becomes divine and godly.

Poetry is what can bring us all together,
Poetry is what can ignite a revolution.
Poetry is what forms the weather,
Poetry with a cause is the real solution.

When you use this *'gift'*,
For your own selfish purposes.
'Tis a gift well wasted, for a perfectly formed rock
    weathers away due to that one gradually formed rift,
And then decomposes.

This is my ode to all those humble poets,
Who are long gone,
And many of whom have been forgotten,
But will always be in our hearts.

The Dead Poets Society, a memory that lives on as we
    revive their sonnets,
Tributes to the Literati of the past will not be enough,
As all those nowadays have become rotten.
Nowadays, the span of attention of a reader is as low as
    the writer's theme of choice charts.

It is all about projecting and putting on the act,
Not about the real ideas of today that influence our
    tomorrow.
It is just an easy way to find people to attract,
So this farce can enhance your ego, indeed a terrible
    sorrow.

If this is forever going to be the case,
Then let us just face the harsh reality-
You are not worthy of poetry.
WE are not worthy of poetry.

For us, it is all about the chase and the race,
Not about ideas of brilliance produced by prose,
Though, these poets work at a slow pace.
For a poet must reap what he/she sows.

For this is my ode to the written word-

Dear poetic license,
You are too gullible to know this, but your excitement
    to enhance language,
Has left a deformity in your appearing presence,
For there is no more a concept of your holy patronage.

Dear literary devices,
You are overused and overburdened,

Like that of an overworked labourer while there is an
    attempt on the part of the manager to cover his
    vices,
I pity you, you are incessantly trampled upon, for now,
    your heart has hardened.

Dear rhyme scheme,
Your use has been criticized.
You are now just compared to an overall theme,
And have been underemphasized.

Dear iambic pentameter,
Nowadays, people prefer free verse,
So the use of stressed and unstressed syllables are just
    seen as repeaters,
Your true potential left unrehearsed.

Keats, Whitman, Poe, Wordsworth,
May your souls rise,
To bring a new generation forth,
And give rebirth to the written word.

A CRITIQUE ON THE CRITIC

You can taint the very wings from my back,
With your blackened envy.

You can ruin the piece I artistically mastered,
With your strokes of carelessness.

You can burn the very soles of my feet,
With your fires of arrogance.

You can choose to break my spirit,
With that glass bottleneck of your emotions.

You can scar and scratch my very skin,
With your devious ways that dictate.

You can lash out on paper,
With your whip of prudence.

You can try to tie my fragile hands,
With your judgemental mouth.

You can hide my art in your own backyard,
To deprive its worth of being in public gaze.

You can publicly shame my name,
By naming yourself a *"fine critic"*.

But I sir, refuse to tolerate your outrage,
It is a crime against humanity,

It is an injustice done to society,
To believe your "words of wisdom".

I, sir, shall not stand down,
Just because my taste is not as rich as yours,

I, sir, shall keep my head held humbly high,
Unlike your gloating head while you merely monetise.

I shall refuse to lick the wounds of society,
While you continue to glorify the disparity.

Look-

I'm sorry if I don't follow your pattern,
Your pattern of monotonous uniformity,

That latches, leeches, and slowly kills,
Till death, for this is an absurdity.

I'm sorry,

I don't match the accuracy of The Maestros,
With my mellifluous, yet enigmatic flow.

I'd rather be seen as risky, not mundane,
I R.E.F.U.S.E T.O. B.E. A. B.O.R.E.

I am sorry,

That I simply cannot orchestrate,
While you sit on that balcony looking for bait.

I am sorry,

That your imagination can't conceive,
The artist's special weave.

I am sorry,

That your backyard is slowly turning into,
A gallery with all my art up for sale.

My crafts may not be crafted,
For those like you.

My skill may be debated and doubted,
By those like you.

There may be perfections in imperfection,
There may be melancholy in what is unnecessarily
    cheerful.

There may be a pattern that confuses,
Rather than reflect on what one chooses.

There may be dark elements,
That are highlighted, rather than shaded.

There may be a mistake on the part of the team,
That is not part of the real dance routine.

But at least, my creativity is original.
And not a replicated version of your values.

Oh, and by the way,

Your values are set nowhere close to reality,
So here's your feedback – your criticism should fall in
    the below-average category.

You rely too much on a portrait, on a script,
On a frame, on a clip,

On a structure, on a format,
On an opinionated diplomat,

On a carving, on a disk,
On some godforsaken book or list,

And this "book" of yours,
Determines my future as an artist?

You expect me to abide by rules that define,
Like solitary confinement, a prison cell.

You expect me to edit expression?
To make stanzas rhyme, to brush up a lullaby,

To make it easier to comprehend,
But also add a touch of zen.

To make landscapes in portrait,
But to also keep it proportionate.

To make my body flexible enough,
To also give it a feminine touch.

Now forgive me for the language,
But please shove these goddamn rules up where they
    belong.

Because you sir, you sir, are a fraud—
You are a liar.

You are a cheat.
You are a manifestation of deceit.

Since when have you possessed all that there is to know?
Do you actually know The Greats and not just by their
    name?

By every stroke, by every note?
By every step, by every word?

By every harmony, by every symphony?
By every synchronised rhythmic melody?

By every brush, by every crease?
By every horizon, by every breeze?

By every metre, by every scheme?
By every passage, by every theme?

Do you truly know what it is to be an artist?
Or are you just some sadistic thief?

You have the audacity to call yourself a critic,
But have you ever questioned yourself as rather a mimic?

Listen, I hate to break it to you.

And I'm sorry to tell you that one day,
My name will be ingrained in stone.

As a painter, a poet, a dancer, a musician,
Or a freedom fighter, a writer in composition.

But you will be forgotten,
As one who dared to call the producer "pathetic".

For you will be despised by many,
For making a farce out of freedom.

Expression is not just in words, you see.
It's in those minds with creativity.

You stifle those free-flowing thoughts,
Which should be considered a deplorable act.

You force magicians to use not a hat,
But rather, an outdated torn thinking cap.

You endorse that the cap is your credit,
Yet still, don't hold back from firing the bullet?

You wicked thieves!
You there, sir, are the epitome of the potbellied nobility!

Sooner or later, you will have to realise,
That millions of masses will want art to be restored.

That's when true freedom will come.
When all will refuse to stand down,

To the dictators of today,
Who prefer filling their pockets by imposing a say.

Art is not what you have made it into,
It exists for humans to explore.

Art doesn't have to be all gold,
Popularity can come from the bold.

Art just has to fulfil its purpose,
To inspire one to grow.

For those who aspire to learn from The Greats,
For those who can feel the artistic flow running through
    their veins.

I say-

Let those imaginative juices run wild,
Let those introspective thoughts run free from fear.

For critics rationalize, but artists dramatize,
Learn to accept Art simply as it is.

For Art was, is, and will be.
For we are born from the imaginary.

Immortal be those souls who reject rigidity,
For we humans should be known to question…

…And not critique.

AN ODE TO THE COMEDIAN

Ladies and Gentlemen,
Put your hands together for all those talented artists out
      there,

Whose cackling sounds,
Are enough to make audiences laugh.

Whose wise use of wit,
Beguiles one to think beyond the horizons.

Whose genuine guilts and fears of life,
Are projected as personal jokes.

Whose professions are to differentiate,
The fine line from freedom of speech.

Humour, what is humour?
Is it merely an eventful enactment?

No, for it is Catharsis through projection.
It is that one moment of happiness after rejection.

Laughter, the best medicine.
A dosage much needed by thousands of those who suffer
    from Depression.

Laughter, the Detoxification of the Soul,
Much needed in this World of Gloom and Doom.

Humour releases the Sanguine,
As amusement rushes into our bloodstream.

It is the Ancient World of Plautine Puns,
And Horatian Satire.

It is the Archaic Comedy of Errors,
And Medieval Comedy of Manners.

It is Dante's Divine Comedy,
And La Comedie Humaine.

That all tied together form a miraculous marvel,
And this marvel is called Comedy.

The emotion certainly captures it all,
As we laugh till on the ground, we fall.

Ridicules arouse all.
Nonsense excites all.

Slapstick surprises all.
Parody pleases all.

Romance serenades all.
The Darkness hauntfully embraces all.

The martyrs then shall always be,
Those who blatantly agree.

It is in the unsaid because sadly,
Some detest truths more than any lie or parody.

The hurtful truths that cannot be swallowed,
By neither minister nor media.

And among all those torturous lies manufactured,
It is those personal stories that must be protected.

Dearest Humour,
Humanity chooses to deconstruct you.

History chooses to convert you.
Politics chooses to subdue you.

You are taken completely out of context,
To mean something you never intended to mean.

The sheer brilliance of a few,
Are set back by someone else who writes a harsh review.

The dedication towards You, the Art,
Shall never remain the same, for you have been broken
     apart,

Into a billion pieces,
Like shattered glass.

That bleed-out observations of that very blood,
Which is in turn, turned into an entire routine.

Your cries become impressions,
And exotic exclamations.

Your wound becomes your shock,
And your bandage becomes your prop.

For the happiest faces,
Hide the saddest hearts.

Hence, I shall salute you, Humour.
Be it whatever stage name you use.

Your courage is more than anyone could ever ask for.

As long as purity lies in your very core,
The world will come to know of you and adore.

The world will see you on stage,
And within the comforts of home surrounded by those
     of all ages.

Children's lives and households affected,
By not suffering, but innocence and laughter reflected.

That one moment of peace and unity,
Lives with you, oh Laughter!

Giggles, chuckles, loud-sounding snorts,
Where each other's differences are all forgotten.

That my friends, is the sound of laughter,
And that sound is the most beautiful of all.

Here's to all those throughout the centuries,
Who have made us laugh.

LIFE'S ESSENCE

WHO ARE YOU?

Who are you?

Are you a dimmed light?
Or a heightened shadow?

Are you a splashing wave?
Or a serene river?

Are you of heavily mountainous terrain?
Or a structure of a slightly curved hill while we notice
      the fertility of the rain?

Who are you?

Are you a savannah with an assortment of a few trees?
Or a canopy of sweet maple with fallen dried leaves?

Are you a magnolia flower with gentility?
Or vines of bougainvillea with tranquillity?

Are you a lakeside domain with a breezy aura?
Or a countryside scene with compacted flora?

Are you in a frame of realistic significance?
Or a utopian world transcending evanescence?

Are you an opaque blood-red sky?
Or a transparent azure, like the wings of a fly?

Who are you?

Are you a thin brush of perfection?
Or a sculpting tool for enhancing complexion?

Are you a landscape of multicolour?
Or a monochromatic portrait, that may seem duller?

Are you a self-explanatory diorama?
Or a plethora of oil strokes that combine to form a
    canvas panorama?

Are you strokes of a beautiful chaos and marvellous
    catastrophe?
Or strokes of only delight and of scenography?

Life is a journey of a bold and wondrous turmoil,
But also can be an irresistible masterpiece.

This power of making a decision,
Lies in the photographer-like precision,

Whose accuracy is one that all worship,
Dimension further adds character to a camera's chip.

Where a click in the right moment may be theoretically,
    an illusion,
Though, it is equivalent to the strokes of a million.

The power also lies in the delicacy of our fingertip... and
    like Columbus,
Our heart binds us to the explorer's compass.

And it all depends upon,
How we illustrate it.

NATURE'S SILHOUETTE

As darkness envelopes the night sky,
A haunting horizon,
Sways with the shadows,
The outcast outlines one's figure,
Like a boundless ocean's boundaries.

Like the Black Sea,
Salty sands surrender,
To the storms orchestrated by Styx,
Melancholy murders the heart,
As sighs and cries taint the soul.

Joy is just fathomed as folly,
When one is frightened by the fearsome,
Thunderous sounds tremor to cut like thorns,
Amidst howls of the sky or shrieks of waves.
Darkness dwells one to death.

Torn tree trunks,
Weeping leaves,
Blackened branches,

Cumulonimbus clouds,
These patterns picture the dreary dream.

Meanwhile, misty mountains in the morn',
With gleaming and glistening gorges,
As ethereal lights scatter across the sky,
Subtle sparks crackle and rumble,
To cause the transparent effect.

Like a prism, the rain,
Knows its place and time,
As one drop ripples a reservoir,
Which colours the atmosphere,
Giving birth to dead and decaying matter.

Pleasant pastures,
Refreshed roses,
Moistened moulds,
Soft succulent fruits,
Vivid and vibrant vines,

Like the light that threatens the forest,
Or the beams that pierce through it.
Like the rainbow after the rain,
Or the mud meandering through movement.
Its mission, to brighten black backgrounds.

It harbours the evanescent evergreen,
Yet also the blurry unforeseen,

It fosters statues of old,
Along with the dilapidated haze,
Wind currents cleanse with their cycle.

Oh, Rain!
You are the true elixir of Earth!
Your canopy stiffens shoots of Oak,
Your family nurtures and nourishes,
And as you fall, we rise as dervishes.

Nature nurtures you,
Tribals worship you,
Dancers express you,
Musicians harmonize you,
Poets pay their tributes to you.

While Painters picture you,
As landscapes become escapades,
You become the yin and the yang,
Your presence radiates throughout sceneries,
Yet shares symbolism with shade.

Oh, Mighty Rain of Heaven and of Hell,
You are nature's alluring silhouette.

DEAREST CAPTAIN

Oh dear captain my captain,
Sail towards the shore of destiny,
Where I am the fire that ignites within.

Sail towards the waves of tranquillity,
Where the whole world shall be your oyster,
And you shall be the precious pearl.

Navigate towards the sun where it shall set,
Where we complete our travels,
And where a new dawn shall arise.

Sail towards the feather of light,
Where all fathom the exit of darkness,
And where life rejuvenates yet again.

Sail with all your might and power,

By helping the engine master its skills,
By holding the engine together,
And by lubricating it with tender care.

Yours truly
A dignified sailor

As the letter was read out to the captain,
Who was adored by all for his humility,
And for being a passionate pioneer.

He chose to answer by appealing to vagabonds with his
    words of wisdom-

"Oh, my fellow companions!

'Tis not I
Who ought to be your leader.
First and foremost, you ought to perceive yourself
As the captain of your own ship.

You shall make yourself worthy,
Teach all lessons in plenty,
Preach them while seeing the clarity,
And feel all senses that are earthy.

Second, fight till your last breath.
It shall be a journey that you must embrace.

Fear not the terror lest you will be kept in disgrace.
So you must earn the right to pass all struggles till you
    arrive at your desired place.

Third, must you forever live with dignity,
Even if you lose your sanity,
And remember,

For it is the core mind that is your true navigator.
For it is the heart that is your true sailor.
For I have realized oh dear ones,
That your true captain lies within.

So oh my fellow companions,
Instead, must you say-
Oh dear captain
Guide me to wherever you desire!"

BITTERSWEET SYMPHONY

The woo of the skies,
The swish of the wind,
The hum of the trees,
The chorus of the birds,
The patter of the rain,
The splash of the oceanic tide,
The silence of the deep-sea mammals,
The harmonic resonance of the hills,

The yodel of the peasants working on the fields,
The folk beats of the forest dwellers,
The soulful taps displayed by the dancers,
The rock genre scaled notes displayed by the bodybuilders,
The opera-like cries for the mourning of the dead,
The cacophonic raps of the protesters,

From major to minor in the change of chords,
From crescendo down back to the lows,
And then back up again,

All are the melodies of life.
And these minor melodies are all synchronized into the
    major scheme of things,
To form this bittersweet symphony.

A SOUL'S METAMORPHOSIS

The journey of the soul,
Is like a Bildungsroman,
Where the protagonist,
Challenges fatal destiny,
To rise in spirit.

And travel
Wide and far,
Till it reaches the limit,
Of this vast universe...
If there even is one.

The soul,
Oversees its
Life and death,
It witnesses the
Skies and Depth.

Solidarities form,
As spiritual guides,
And omnipresent ancestors,

All sing tunes to illuminate paths,
To navigate the soul self to its being.

The soul envisions the shades of life,
Where the prophetic vision of the soul,
Highlight sceneries, caressed by all,
Before stepping into the realms of darkness,
Here, experientiality becomes sentimentality.

The predestined soulless life that is meant,
To be challenged and altered by the soul.
For the soul must continue its' voyage,
By evoking its creativity of the self.

After all, it is they who survive the ravages of time.

Therefore, the soul must make life arduous,
And torment one's being into submission,
Or prostrate one before a higher power,
To remind the human race of their inferiorities.

Growth, too, can be seen as transcendental,
The soul experiences many versions of life,
From that of a pauper to a merchant,
Or from a merchant to that of a pauper,

It overcomes its battles with depression,
Just like the collective does.

It succumbs to being numb as mired minds,
Just like the collective does.
To search for the true version of the self.

It overshadows the devastation,
To watch the being find its way back,
To the soul, that is lost in the labyrinth.
It also casts its light on others, like a torch,
To guide those spiritless beings lost at sea.

The soul educates itself,
To become the Tree of Oak,
Grounded in intellect and innocence,
Bloomed in a history of curiosities and uncertainties,
Branched in various epiphanies of the mind, body, and
    consciousness.

A mystery to the Unknown,
When their seeds of life remain sown,
Yet their fulfilled duties continue to spark joy,
While their unfulfilled ones, dissipate,
Dissipate...into nothingness.

Experimentation with emotions,
Is the rightful duty of a soul,
Where life must confuse the being,
To behave irrationally, like Love,
Or the essence of survival of the species.

From animal to human,
And human to animal,
From animal or insect to plant,
And plant to animal or insect,
The circle of life and evolution entirely explored.

Ultimately, it is the many lives lived,
Where the caterpillar of a soul,
Metamorphoses into a butterfly-like glow,
The brighter it shines, the higher it elevates.

Till it reaches the far end of the Cosmos,
The goal of every soul, therefore,
To become enlightened,
To seek silence,
In its Death.

A MESSAGE OF FAITH

A force field surrounds you,
A shield is what defends you,
Though there is no turning back,
There is no running off-track.

You are destined to survive,
You are determined to revive,
So must you not pester yourselves with the race against
    time,
For "it is how well you live that matters, not how long",
    as said by a Latin rhyme.

You were the messiahs of the past,
As you took on the struggle till your very last,
And synchronized the bright minds,
To emit a light as bright as yours that binds.

You are the ones with the gifted halo of the present,
You hold ideals of virtue true to yourself that many may
    resent,
You are the colour of the pleasant skies,
Where harmonious existence is what flies.

You are the fighters of tomorrow,
For it starts by letting go of your previous sorrows,
Your patience will be tested,
Though your tolerance will stand as still as when crested.

You all have a special power,
If you build on this, you will rise from the dust in the
    form of a blooming flower,
Or like the Phoenix, a bird of mythological history,
That emerges from the ashes like a mystery.

You all are the angels of God,
For you, all can be the mighty Nimrod,
So then, why must you feel tumultuary?
Why must you feel the urge to write your own obituary?

Must you know that-

The law of attraction prevails,
A universal law that never fails.
You all are the centre of the surreal portrait,
So, it is up to you when and how to colour it.

A dimensional stability
Is what determines the accuracy of your predictability.
Where your magnetic resonance
Travels far across the seas of illuminance.

So, rest your faith
On the shores of destiny...

SURRENDER

Dens of despair,
Prisons of paranoia,
Cages of confusion,
Lockdowns of loneliness,

Enclosures of entitlement,
Chambers of chaos,
Zones of malign attainment of zenith,
Jails of jealousy,

Confinements of covetousness,
Dungeons of dictatorship,
Walls of wrath,
Lofty limits of lust,

These are the restrictions that imprison the human soul.
Just like the containment cells of gas,
A toxic terrorism.
Just like the maladaptive misers,
Who cling to worldly possessions.
Just like a venus flytrap,
Feeding on parasitic pleasures.

It latches onto you like a creeper,
While finding yourself drops deeper.
For once you use these emotions to wrap
...Around, you fall into a terrible trap.

The real discovery
Of your spirit's journey,
Your connect with otherworldly presences
Can only happen
Once your visions are focused not on this world,
But on your "self".

Attainment of enlightenment
Is what your purpose in life is.
It applies to each one of you.
Though you needn't renounce like the Buddha did,
For temptation exists, as a worldly virtue Temptation of
     religiosity too, a worldly virtue.
So, use your senses wisely,
And renounce only what must be renounced.

Commence your journey,
By surrendering your past sins,
And abandon the ideas of despair, paranoia, confusion,
     loneliness,
Abandon the behaviours of entitlement, abuse, and
     misuse, jealousy,
Abandon greed, anger, and lust.

Walk on the islands of the immaterial,
Travel to the times of transcendental,
Float on the calm seas of the spiritual,

And surrender yourself to God.
Surrender....surrender yourself to God.

THE PILGRIMAGE OF LIFE

Life, a voyage,
As you make us travel across the seven seas,
As we battle the waves of depression,
And as we climb up the docks of happiness.

Oh, life!

The tempests thrown in my face,
To tumble me over into a vertigo,
The ships that almost sink,
As you challenge the waters to fight back.

The raging fires of hell,
That engulfs even water,
The dried-out rivers, all soaked up,
That breaks us into burnout.

The tremors to terrorize all,
As you hope I don't fall into despair,
The departed winds that deceive,
As you calm all into a stillness,

Are all overturned, by my faith.

Life,

Death is afraid of you.
As the closer it comes,
You forge ahead as fearless and reckless,
You metamorphosise one even before death approaches.

But I am not afraid.
I am not worried.
I know I won't flinch before my demise.
I know I won't cry in fear of my life.

Time tests me,
Just like you test me,
And as I test these waters,
Even perceptional illusions hoodwink me.

You force me to forage and hunt,
I happily become your slave,
And beat my back till you are done with me.
For you are my master, my one true teacher.

You kick me into the deep end,
To strengthen my core, my lungs, my breath,
So I shall not forget how to swim ever again.
For I must learn to face the rapids of survival.

You push me to be at least an inch away,
From the edge of a cliff,
So I am left hanging,
To know what 'almost falling' feels like.

You toss poisonous vipers,
And treacherous snakes my way,
To test my patience in these toxic times,
To mirror a snake, simultaneously, to hold still.

You jolt me into shocks of great magnitude,
So the turbulence of energies,
eventually, won't affect my grounding,
The lesson is how to become at one with the universe.

You shove me into the paths of shade,
To remind me, how it feels to walk in the dark,
And that my delicate touch can save souls,
The moment the darkness corrodes.

Oh, life! My master!

Just like you taught me,
I refuse to give up now.
I refuse to fall and crumble onto the ground.
Rather, I will continue to let you interrogate me.

The long distances travelled,
The thousands of hearts comforted,

The natural realm that lays before us,
And the realms, yet to be conquered.
All worth the suffering.

No sip, no morsel that ever has touched my lips,
No pain, no slit that has ever wounded me so,
For I shall continue my quest,
With or without your help.

In search of the beauty, I call, life.

THE ESSENCE OF SENESCENCE

When you're old enough to be pure,
And pure enough to be old.

When time is baffled with your existence,
And your existence grapples with the question of time.

When your perception grows like a tree,
And the tree's seed imbibes introspection.

When your history speaks of your present,
And the present studies of your history.

When lights are refractive of the dark,
And the darkness reflects the light.

When the summer fields grow in the spring,
And spring colours the season of summer.

When long nights call for Dawn,
And Dusk summons the moon.

When from the rain, a fire burns,
And that same fire sparks it to rain.

When clouds hover and cover the sun,
And sun rays scatter light even in the clouds.

When journeys transcend to the spiritual,
And when spirits descend to lift your adventurous soul.

When old age is your pause, your comma,
And not your full stop.

When the youth is told the tales of ole,
And ancient oral tales are retold by the youth.

When statues decay and books omit your narrative,
Yet your narrative, powerful enough to tear those
    pompous statues down.

Your voice may be soft and weak,
Yet your wise words are heard loud and clear.

Your eyes, despite being incongruous with the sensation,
Blessed may you be with the gift of insight.

Your ears require an aid to apprehend all,
Yet faint echoes of the past are heard by you, and you
    alone.

When a sundry of smells distorts your senses,
Yet you sense the petrichor before the rain.

When your warm soul leaves your cold body,
Yet the body eternally remembers your soul.

When life announces your death,
And death prophesizes a new life,

That is the essence of senescence.